BARODA

A Cosmopolitan Provenance

in Transition

BARODA

A Cosmopolitan Provenance

in Transition

edited by
Priya Maholay-Jaradi

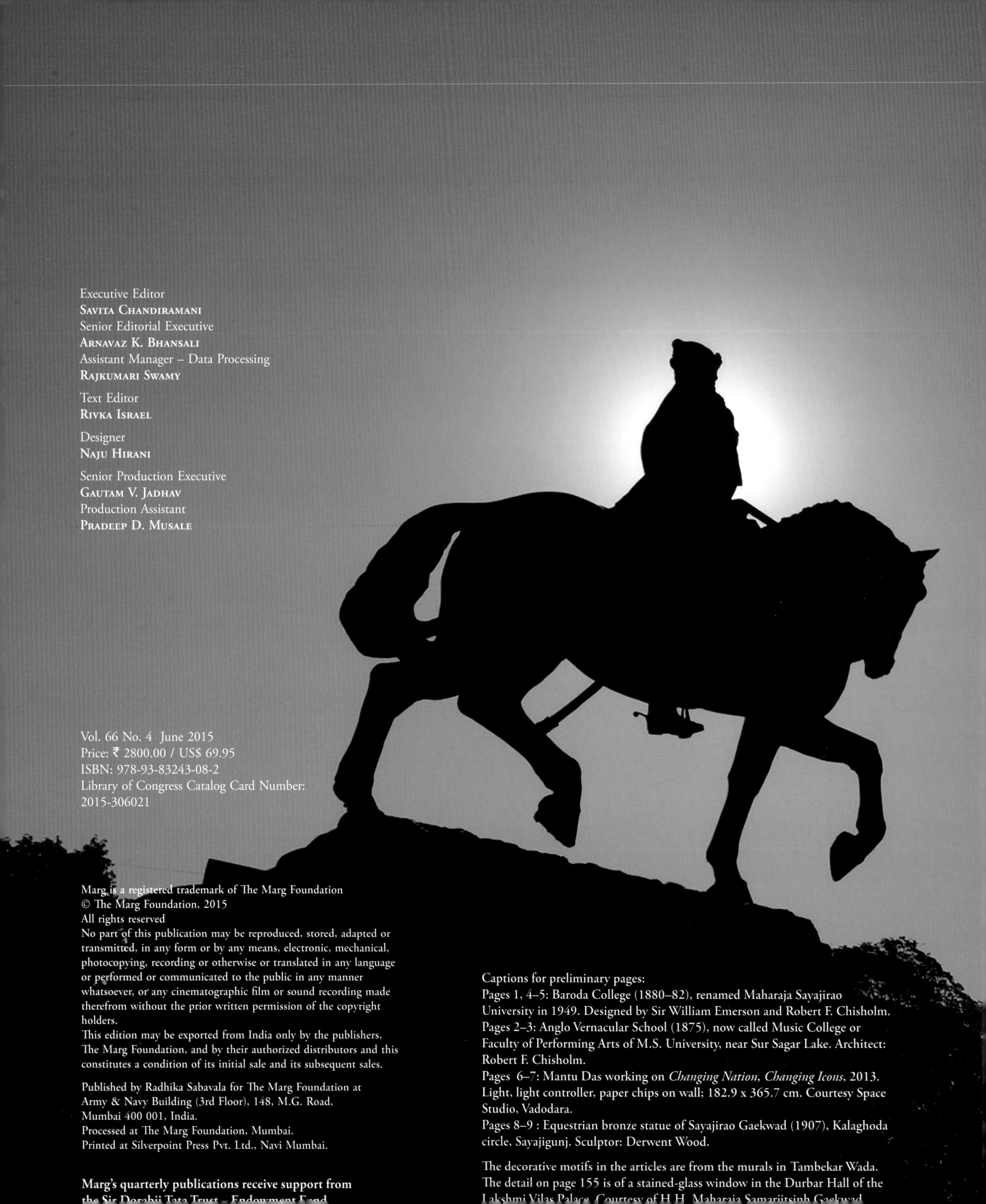

Executive Editor
Savita Chandiramani
Senior Editorial Executive
Arnavaz K. Bhansali
Assistant Manager – Data Processing
Rajkumari Swamy

Text Editor
Rivka Israel

Designer
Naju Hirani

Senior Production Executive
Gautam V. Jadhav
Production Assistant
Pradeep D. Musale

Vol. 66 No. 4 June 2015
Price: ₹ 2800.00 / US$ 69.95
ISBN: 978-93-83243-08-2
Library of Congress Catalog Card Number:
2015-306021

Marg is a registered trademark of The Marg Foundation
© The Marg Foundation, 2015
All rights reserved
No part of this publication may be reproduced, stored, adapted or
transmitted, in any form or by any means, electronic, mechanical,
photocopying, recording or otherwise or translated in any language
or performed or communicated to the public in any manner
whatsoever, or any cinematographic film or sound recording made
therefrom without the prior written permission of the copyright
holders.
This edition may be exported from India only by the publishers,
The Marg Foundation, and by their authorized distributors and this
constitutes a condition of its initial sale and its subsequent sales.

Published by Radhika Sabavala for The Marg Foundation at
Army & Navy Building (3rd Floor), 148, M.G. Road,
Mumbai 400 001, India.
Processed at The Marg Foundation, Mumbai.
Printed at Silverpoint Press Pvt. Ltd., Navi Mumbai.

**Marg's quarterly publications receive support from
the Sir Dorabji Tata Trust – Endowment Fund**

Captions for preliminary pages:
Pages 1, 4–5: Baroda College (1880–82), renamed Maharaja Sayajirao
University in 1949. Designed by Sir William Emerson and Robert F. Chisholm.
Pages 2–3: Anglo Vernacular School (1875), now called Music College or
Faculty of Performing Arts of M.S. University, near Sur Sagar Lake. Architect:
Robert F. Chisholm.
Pages 6–7: Mantu Das working on *Changing Nation, Changing Icons*, 2013.
Light, light controller, paper chips on wall; 182.9 x 365.7 cm. Courtesy Space
Studio, Vadodara.
Pages 8–9 : Equestrian bronze statue of Sayajirao Gaekwad (1907), Kalaghoda
circle, Sayajigunj. Sculptor: Derwent Wood.

The decorative motifs in the articles are from the murals in Tambekar Wada.
The detail on page 155 is of a stained-glass window in the Durbar Hall of the
Lakshmi Vilas Palace. Courtesy of H.H. Maharaja Samarjitsinh Gaekwad.

Contents

Unless otherwise credited,
photographs by Manish Chauhan.

Foreword

For almost a decade in the 1980s and '90s, a group of us undertook a project to research the art scene of Baroda. This resulted in the publication of the book *Contemporary Art in Baroda* in 1997. Essentially our objective, as well as the brief from our sponsors, was to chronicle the establishment and growth of an art school in a non-metropolitan city, one which had emerged as a prominent institution on the national art scene with an international outreach. The ambitious educational initiative which charged the Faculty of Fine Arts (FFA) in Baroda was supported by the newly founded Maharaja Sayajirao University of Baroda that pioneered the introduction of the fine arts (assumedly a "soft" discipline) on a par with the hard sciences and technology within the university system. This was perceived as part of the agenda of nation-building in the early years of Independence.

Our endeavour to study a local contemporary art scene in the context of the post-Independence nation drew us to the antecedents of art practice in the erstwhile princely state of Baroda. Uncovering layers of what had initially seemed to be an amorphous past, revealed multiple areas of art practice from the late-18th century onwards. Our survey of murals began with religious structures such as the Kashi Vishwanath temple in the small town of Chandod (1782 CE) and the facades and interiors of numerous domestic buildings of the mofussil towns of Baroda state. This uncovered the presence of a wider visual culture spread over urban and semi-urban provenances continuing right up to Independence. The city murals of Tambekar Wada from the mid-19th century, and the Kirti Mandir walls painted by Nandalal Bose in the early 1940s, opened doors to other kinds of art practice. Accounts of visiting artists and scholars brought into view the seminal role Baroda played in the career of Raja Ravi Varma. Baroda also provided the opportunity to the emigre Indologist Hermann Goetz to build a collection of world art, using copies where originals were not available, for an exemplary museum of art history in the city. Art-historical discourse was initiated through the Museum bulletin. Our research revealed these and, tantalizingly, other potential areas to investigate, in the princely, civic and religious sectors. The limitations of time and resources at our disposal prompted our decision to concentrate on tracing the art scene as it unfolded in the decades following Independence.

Every book with any claim to historicity would aspire to an afterlife; *Contemporary Art in Baroda* too awaited further footfalls in the subject it had covered. It is heartening that the spaces it opened resulted in the project *Baroda: A Cosmopolitan Provenance in Transition*. The former initiative had attempted to discuss the progression of an art scene (while also marking a year-by-year timeline of events from 1731 to 1994) and had involved four contributors who commented on broadly chronological phases. The 12 contributors of the present volume have put their minds to unravelling intricate discourses in art practice and art-historical pedagogy in and around the provenance of Baroda. Outlining the thematic concern, Ajay Sinha, one of the contributors, writes: "... provenance helps build historical depth and material density into the interpretation of modern and contemporary art."

Some of the contributions in this volume can be said to be expanding the earlier ground, filling in gaps or exploring in depth previously briefly charted areas. Calling upon the initiative of building a visual archive as a pedagogical aid in Baroda (with reference

Kalabhavan, Maharaja Sayajirao University, Baroda.

to a similar and earlier practice in Santiniketan) Chithra K.S., Rashmimala Devi and Sabih Ahmed in their joint essay enlarge the idea of the archive beyond its stereotypical objectives. They emphasize that "archives constitute the practice and parameters of discourse, not just represent it." A detailed account affirms that "Baroda's pedagogy that began as an experiment led to artists and art historians creating an epistemological means to redraw (and rewrite) art-historical lineages afresh."

However, in most instances the primary engagement has been with theoretical discourse around the problematics of art production within the mutations of a changing socio-political scenario. Ajay Sinha makes an in-depth analysis of what he calls the "princely modernity" which characterizes Baroda's visual culture. He recounts how Dadasaheb Phalke, at the beginning of his career, performed the dual roles of photographer and magician, using the magical "trickery" of photography to overcome the prevalent superstition that a photograph shortens the subject's life. Interestingly this photographic trickery was "a forerunner of his breakthrough in Indian cinema, where he made gods come alive on the movie screen". Chaitanya Sambrani has taken an insider's view of the city, beginning with a gastronomic metaphor to articulate a critique that contests the provenance of Baroda as a site. Examining the heterogeneous mix that Baroda represents, he finds that it is formed of isolated networks, its provincial location set against what he calls "aspirational cosmopolitanism". Santhosh Sadanand extends the argument in his incisive analysis of the art scene to question the claim of Baroda as a provenance to a cosmopolitan ethos. He chooses the decade from 1999 onwards to substantiate his indictment of the city for its absence of a "community" and the failures of praxis and discourse in realizing and responding to the rising spectre of violence and majoritarianism. Deeptha Achar takes the argument further, problematizing the complex relationship of art practice within the various orbits of the FFA with its viewing public, in the context of the events of 2007 and thereafter. Finally, in a broad summing up, Shivaji Panikkar has narrated the historical scenario with its political underpinnings that have affected current art practice and pedagogy at the FFA.

Other contributions chart somewhat different courses. Undivided focus on the artists N.S. Bendre and Jyoti Bhatt and their art practice marks the essays by Ratan Parimoo and Karin Zitzewitz respectively. Parimoo's fond recounting of the time he learnt from his teacher Bendre, of the closely observed "demonstrations" of how to draw or paint a still-life or life-study evokes the performative act of the master-painter, which seems to follow the traditional guru-shishya system of pedagogy through personal mode of work. In a similar vein Parimoo locates the cubist experiments of Bendre in the Indian context, citing his colourful palette as drawn from Indian miniatures, and suggesting the attribution of both to the bright "Indian" sunshine. In order to define the raison d'etre of Jyoti Bhatt's photographic and printmaking practice Zitzewitz reconstructs his long engagement with the documentation of vanishing traditions of the Indian village. She searches for the sources of this passion within the ambit of his Gandhian background and the cultural-nationalism of northern Gujarat that guided his education and his passage into the discovery of indigenous cultures, rather than within the current idea of the "modern" at Baroda. She also sees a close connection between Gujarati litterateur Jhaverchand Meghani's lifelong research on the oral archives of indigenous knowledge and Bhatt's visual documentation, in "collecting as well as rehabilitating ... folk knowledge". In an exclusive analysis of the architectural legacy of Baroda, Christopher London considers the work of Robert Chisholm and Charles Mant. His reading of the traditional Marathi wada house design as the basis of early palace structures gives the work of these two seminal builder-architects of colonial India provincial antecedents. London provides a detailed account of the Baroda palaces, their interiors and structural components – in the case of the recently demolished Nazarbaug Palace, this would now read as an elegy.

The process of conducting this book project became a conference of sorts between the contributors and editor, with an exchange of ideas on a variety of issues. The detailed point-by-point discussions, including the ways in which arguments are articulated, provide a rich fare of ideas of convergence and difference. I found the continued debate on email most rewarding; obviously, yet sadly, this could not form part of the publication. In her own essay on Baroda at colonial exhibitions, editor Priya Maholay-Jaradi discusses the continuous involvement of the state of Baroda, and of Sayajirao III in particular, in "a cosmopolitical worldview ... produced through aesthetics" and builds a narrative around exhibits presented at "international" exhibitions from the mid-19th century onwards. Her essay provides the ground on which several contributors have built their arguments. She formulates the claim of Baroda as a provenance with an interface of the provincial and the cosmopolitan, which created "the cultural condition in which local modes of production and consumption dialogue with globally hegemonic forms and networks".

It may appear, in retrospect, that there is an implicit lament or anxiety over the loss of a cosmopolitan legacy in the last two decades – or even a suggestion that its presence is arguable in the first place. Yet, within this very critique there is a call for redressal. The argumentative value of this careful but impassioned discourse is enhanced by the views of the city from inside set in an interface with views taken from outside, from a perspectival distance in time and place. And there is room for further readings that approach Baroda from "all four cardinal points" as well as leave it "from all these points", as Santhosh says, quoting Walter Benjamin.

Gulammohammed Sheikh
Vadodara, 2015

BARODA/VADODARA

to Ahmedabad

to Anand

SAMA

NH 11

KARELIBAUG

• Methodist Church

PRATAPGUNJ   FATEHGUNJ

ALKAPURI

M.S. UNIVERSITY

University Road

FFA   SAYAJIGUNJ

Railway Station•

NH 11

R.C. Dutt Road

•Baroda Museum and Picture Gallery

Sayaji   Kalaghoda Circle

Clocktower   Kirti Mandir

Vinoba Bhave Road

Chimnabai

SSG Hospital•   Clocktower   M.G.   CHHIPWAD

Space Studio•   •   Nagar   Central Library•

Municipal Corporation Office•   Kothi Offices•   Gruh   Nazarbaug Palace•

Jail Road   Tambekar Wada   Leharipura Gate•

DANDIA BAZAR   Sur Sagar Lake   Panigate Road

M.G. Road   Jamnabai

Music College•   •   Hospital•

Ajwa Road

Bhaskarrao Vithal Wada•   Nyaya

Mandir

Old Padra Road   Khanderao Market

Tagore Road

Vaasna-Bhaayli Road

Akota Road

AKOTA   Lakshmi Vilas Palace•

J.N. Road

PALACE GROUNDS

Fatesingh Museum•

Chhaap•

Pratap Vilas Palace•

Vishwamitri river

LALBAUG

to Mumbai

Sussen Tarsali Ring Road

to Bharuch

MAKARPURA

Makarpura Palace•   Tarsali Lake

Sketch-map, not to scale

Introduction

Priya Maholay-Jaradi

This volume is conceived against the busy backdrop of a recasting of the discipline of art history, which has been underway in the last two decades in postcolonial nation-states such as India. The discipline earlier enjoyed a predominantly Eurocentric formulation which gave it a few primary characteristics: First, Western standards were applied to judge non-Western artistic practices; in the absence of indigenous contexts to appreciate African and Asian arts, they were either understood as being primitive or non-scientific. Second, modern art experiments were seen as *derivative* of their Western counterparts and thought to enjoy a very late arrival in *peripheral* geographies of the colonies vis-a-vis the perceived *centre*, i.e. the West. Third, indigenous arts were seen as representing *national* culture, which was perceived to be at odds with *colonial* (read European) art practices. And last, this emphasis on homogeneous national categories saw a less nuanced understanding of smaller, provincial schools. This Eurocentric art history promoted dichotomies such as centre-periphery, national-colonial, national-provincial and pure/modern-derivative;[1] in contrast, the current recasting of art history chooses to collapse these dichotomies and present their domains as negotiating and constituting each other.

The new approach has secularized art-historical enquiry to make it more inclusive of genres, practices, locations and production periods which may have otherwise been a part of dichotomous domains and their rigid understandings. Moreover, these diverse genres may emerge from different socio-political contexts such as the colonial, national, post-national and pan-Asian, and yet have the potential to be reconfigured through alternative themes in what has been called a "New Art History" by Shivaji Panikkar and his colleagues at the Faculty of Fine Arts (FFA), Maharaja Sayajirao University of Baroda, since early 2000.[2] Aligning with the new art history, the provincial location of Baroda and its visual culture spanning c. 1700–2015 is spotlighted in this volume through alternative themes of cosmopolitanism and provenance.

In keeping with the tradition of profiling a cultural centre, this volume could have been a compilation of essays which discuss Baroda as a city and its heritage;[3] however one overhauls this format of a "cultural diary" to locate Baroda at multiple intersections: spatial, temporal and geo-political. This is to say that Baroda's career as a centre for the arts spans plural domains: Baroda as a princely state that was culturally groomed by its royal patrons; Baroda as the foremost model of colonial modernity which saw the founding of administrative, art and educational institutions; Baroda at the intersection of the royal and colonial, articulating an alternative modernity and nationalism; Baroda projecting its modernity in independent India; and Baroda today, a hub for contemporary curatorial and art practice and a key chapter in the making of a contemporary Asia Art Archive.[4] Clearly, these overlapping chapters in Baroda's cultural career qualify it as a historical provenance.

The term "provenance" equips us to make that transition from a cultural diary format to an alternative approach. Provenance implies the place of origin or production of an art work/practice. Hence, even if products, practitioners or ideologies negotiate change, the "Baroda provenance" remains. This volume is framed along the twinned axes of "Baroda as a centre for the arts", and the "Baroda provenance": while the former witnesses physical and ideological changes, the latter accrues discursive weight as a constantly evolving, cosmopolitan provenance.

This book primarily differs in its two-pronged approach: the first being to "profile the city" and its growth as an art and culture capital; the second being to approach the city through the lens of "provenance research". In the process, this study unravels plural agencies in the shaping of the city's art and heritage contours and also points to the multiple narratives that the Baroda provenance occupies: art-historical, architectural, pedagogical, curatorial, exhibitionary and archival.[5] Thus, both Barodas, the (empirical) city and the (theoretical) provenance, chart their journey from a provincial princely state to a cosmopolitan centre. Through this study of Baroda the book aims to contribute to new theoretical ideas of provenance and cosmopolitanism among others.

***

Almost two years since the concept outlined above was first laid out, through their stimulating discussions and what Gulammohammed Sheikh recounts in his Foreword as an interface between views taken from inside and outside the city, the contributors seem to be questioning the very premise upon which the anthology was conceived: they argue the loss of Baroda's cosmopolitan inheritance. What began as a progressive maharaja's project of building an inclusive arts' model (alongside a highly inclusive princely state which opposed the caste system, brahmanical orthodoxy and exclusion of women from education) has evolved today as a site with one of the country's best Fine Arts colleges, albeit lately disconnected with the city and its local population, as pointed out by Santhosh S. Thus, a princely state which steadily moved from a royal to a more liberal and plebeian vision, as analysed by Ajay Sinha, ensured participation from diverse registers of the population to construct and represent this provenance. High-art practitioners from overseas, society portraitists and artisans from far afield benefited from royal budgets to represent Baroda internationally during the Raj. The viewing public too was welcomed in the royal precincts of the Durbar Hall at Lakshmi Vilas to view the works of Raja Ravi Varma in 1890–91.

Sayajirao's equestrian statue, Baroda's famous Kalaghoda, viewed against a setting sun reminds us of the demise of princely Indian states through their accession to independent India, then led by the Indian National Congress. Various political parties have periodically displayed retrograde ideologies through violent modes of censorship on freedom of expression and incitement of communal violence. In the last decade, Hindu majoritarian parties chose to redefine the provenance on the basis of exclusion as opposed to a cosmopolitan inclusion of practitioners, ideas and objects. All the same, the courting of capital and modernization continues today at the same pace as set by Maharaja Sayajirao Gaekwad III and Maharani Chimnabai to the unease of the British Parliament.

In his detailed essay discussing the growth of Indo-Saracenic architecture which culminated in buildings such as the grandiose Lakshmi Vilas Palace, Christopher London

1
Sayaji Express, the new toy train at Kamatibaug/Sayajibaug, inaugurated in 2013.

provides an effective pointer to how Indian architectural principles opened up to European resources to later fructify in absorptive design strategies. The *indigenous* was always at the centre of an expanding cosmopolitan activity, which has characterized ideas and the physical cityscape since. This absorptive element and an aversion to the hierarchies of high and low, art and artisanal, global and local, are incisively discussed in Ratan Parimoo and Karin Zitzewitz's essays. The multiplicity of sources and tools employed in art pedagogy, art practice and even the building of archives, and their cross-referencing as discussed by Parimoo, Zitzewitz, Chithra K.S., Rashmimala Devi and Sabih Ahmed, lend a formidable cosmopolitan character to the post-Independence art scene in Baroda. The absolute unhinging of fixities and categories of art schools and their discourses hint at time, change and an evolving city and public sphere.

Markers of such transitions are aplenty in the city. The famous toy train commissioned in 1941 by Maharaja Pratapsinh Gaekwad for his son, Ranjitsinh, to facilitate the prince's daily commute from the Lakshmi Vilas Palace to the school,[6] was opened to the children of the city in 1956.[7] For many of us, as children, a holiday in Baroda was incomplete without a toy train ride at Kamatibaug. Increasing maintenance costs led to the museumization of the original train; in its stead, a new bigger train which can accommodate adults plies since 2013. Changes also abound in the incessant reworking of the old and new. As the Dandiya Bazaar and Raopura Market with streets dedicated to terracotta-ware, dupattas and spices continue to flourish, mega-malls, fast-food eateries and shopping arcades multiply in their vicinity. The Nazarbaug Palace in the heart of the Old City has been recently demolished and Baroda's swankiest mall is announced at the site. A panoramic view of Sur Sagar Lake and its surroundings is indicative of compact old clusters which continue to absorb new buildings, hoardings and neon lights. Google Earth once showed large tracts of land

2
Shree Chimnabai Nyaya Mandir, built in 1896. Once the High Court of Baroda state, it is now the District Court. Architect: Robert F. Chisholm.

3
Kamatibaug/Sayajibaug, opened in 1879, on the banks of the Vishwamitri river.

and waterbodies adjoining Baroda. Today, Vaasna and Bhaayli *villages* are marked with luxury residential complexes, ATM kiosks, colleges and international schools, announcing their arrival as Baroda's new *suburbs*. As Google Earth brings larger tracts of land within Vadodara's cityscape and as the city's municipal limits expand, the shrinking of Baroda's ideological scope and inclusive spirit across the 1980s, '90s and especially in the years 2002 and 2007, is teased out in this volume.

Baroda's time-keepers may be seen metaphorically in the two clocktowers that inhabit the cityscape: the more noticeable Chimnabai Clocktower at the busy market of Raopura and the partially foliage-covered clocktower at Sayajigunj. Perhaps when a member of the Bombay Progressive Artists' Group, A.A. Raiba, painted "Baroda's clocktower", its allure was intact as a central landmark, a historical monument which celebrated enlightened patronage. More importantly, there were enough vantage points to view the tower(s) and appreciate their architecture in a less crowded Baroda then. Even if the painting is not an exact reproduction of either tower but more an impression of both, and even if it is rendered along an inauthentic location of a forked street,[8] the centrality of the clock itself and the idea of progress, time, modernity and an organized city unmistakably occupy Raiba's work. According to Zitzewitz, form adjusts itself in Baroda's modern art experiments; a playful reading of the idea allows us to see the adjustment of form in Raiba's work and, now again, in contemporary photographs of the clocktowers. This time round, form adjusts itself to

4
Old toy train at Kamatibaug.
Commissioned by Maharaja Pratapsinh
Gaekwad in 1941, it was moved to
Kamatibaug in 1956.

temporal shifts, less for any aesthetic reason and more for mundane needs of upkeep and preservation. Raymond's showroom pays rent for occupying the Chimnabai Clocktower, and we climb to the roof-terrace of a shoe shop on the opposite side of the street to get a complete photograph. The Sayaji Clocktower is occupied by a police station.

As we walk back from Raopura, large hoardings of "VadFest",[9] Gujarat Tourism's maiden initiative for Baroda's own festival of the performing and visual arts, are fast going up across the city. Co-passengers travelling on the Shatabdi train to Mumbai discuss booking tickets to watch Yanni against the backdrop of the Lakshmi Vilas. The provenance clearly has a hold over popular imagination and so do its monuments and cultural pursuits. To redeploy Deeptha Achar's idea here, to explain audience patronage for the VadFest as support for cultural-nationalism or any political party would mean reducing the significance of the very different visual universe which is constantly at play in the public sphere. Yanni, A.R. Rahman and Nandita Das are stalwarts from the performing arts scene who induce verve in the popular imagination.

But what is more relevant to our context of discussion is the component of visual arts: India's top artists (often alumni of the FFA, Baroda), students and faculty members at the FFA participate in VadFest as artists or curators. A steady stream of letters, columns and posts on social media and email call on all participants to withdraw support from VadFest, hosted by a government which attacked the freedom of expression of a student at the FFA in 2007, leading to the unceremonious suspension of the Dean and denial of an arts degree to the student. Instances of communal riots in Baroda as well as such interventions by political parties, especially the majoritarian groups at the FFA, have led to the questioning of Baroda's cosmopolitanism in the later chapters of this book. All the same, the current state of Baroda's art fraternity and the FFA as an isolated, hermetic and even romantic lot is underlined by Santhosh and Achar. The public's increasing support of the majoritarian political groups is palpable since 2007, when the artist community fought a lone battle.

Given these cross-currents which grip Baroda today, one sadly admits that the provenance has split into two or perhaps three: one being nurtured by what is perceived as an "elite"

5
Sur Sagar Lake, formerly Chandan Talao. Stone banks were built around the lake in the mid-18th century, at which time it was renamed.

and self-admittedly left-leaning artists'/academic community; another being courted by a majoritarian rightwing (political) community; and a third liberal group, which, as per an eyewitness account, supported the artists' community and the student victim in 2007.[10] As agency to decide the future of this provenance is equally fragmented, it becomes ever more necessary to ask if withdrawing from VadFest is a solution to garner support for freedom of expression and secure a more secular outlook in the city. For, if VadFest is about unprecedented visitor numbers and footfall in Baroda and if the FFA is characterized by a self-constructed exclusivity today, then connecting the two domains is crucial towards rebuilding the lost sociality between artists and the viewing public, as highlighted by Achar and Panikkar.

VadFest can be that meeting ground which helps to grow an informed, visually proficient art-going audience; it can become that space where the visual universe of the artist community overlaps with that of the audiences to bridge the widening gap between the two. With systematic public art education by the fine-arts community, there is hope that over a few editions of VadFest, the viewing public will assess and appreciate an art work on its own terms. It will not scrutinize the works through the lens of a politically charged and biased space. After all, museums and museum fraternities across the world do not necessarily enjoy governments with whom they affiliate ideologically; moreover as non-revenue-generating agencies, they are compelled to function closely with the elected government's agencies, but what they do achieve in the long run is to cultivate museum-going audiences.

It is relevant here to cite Shekhar Gupta's persuasive piece which points to how post-Independence India often forgets that liberal constituencies are made of a liberal right and a liberal left; the liberal left has often "artfully" and sometimes "crudely" pushed out the liberal right, to the extent that the latter is now embraced by the extreme right.[11] Gupta emphasizes the elitism of the liberal left's material, social and intellectual leanings; so also, the art community has become a liberal-left monopoly, at least in its intellectual and social manifestations.[12] It is time for this community to artfully embrace citizens of this provenance and beyond to cultivate them as visually proficient audiences rather than to see their responses being modulated by political instruments. After all, Chaitanya Sambrani's theoretically grounded arguments tell us that cosmopolitanism may be understood in two ways: laying claim for belonging to a larger territory or making your own territory/ self hospitable to outsiders. And if, historically, the FFA has been hospitable to represent the multiplicity of the Indian nation-state as Panikkar reminds us, it can represent the multiplicity of viewers with which it has the potential to connect; it can also represent a multiplicity of visual universes which it can build with specialists, generalists and a large mass of the public.

The Chimnabai Clocktower wears a dial with Roman numerals and the Sayaji Clocktower displays one with Devanagari lipi (script). Maharani Chimnabai and Maharaja Sayajirao's art projects were about fielding the cross-currents of foreign styles and media with indigenous practices to redefine a new national art. And that spirit of inclusion was based on pragmaticism, effectively pointed out by Sinha. Perhaps the arts fraternity needs to make that shift from the romantic to the pragmatic; for, otherwise, not only will the physical and ideological space of Baroda cease to field new currents, but even the "indigenous" will be redefined from a narrow, ill-informed visual universe; one that cannot appreciate the full sophistication of a civilization[13] and its previous, more erudite and assimilative waves of cultural-nationalisms.

In closing, one returns to locate this volume's provenance approach in Baroda's contemporary context. The city's vibrant markets, malls, arts festivals and the general celebration of capital should not be mistaken as the ultimate contemporary expression of the provenance. One will see how provenance becomes a methodological tool to build historical depth throughout the volume, as Sinha will tell us. Provenance renders a diachronic history of Baroda: it helps to substantiate Baroda's princely precedents in the artistic sphere and their shaping of latter-day antecedents; at the same time it demonstrates how later traditions regenerate themselves and remain rooted by referencing historical and contemporary practices. The broad time-frames made possible by the provenance approach serve as reminders of a meaningful coexistence of previous spectacular booms brought by capital and modernization and the many ideas of secularism, inclusion and egalitarianism which were practised alongside. It is important, then, that provenance serves as a critical mode to retrieve the memories and character of a historical provenance, lest Baroda's current artistic expressions become ahistorical and a mere spectacle.

6

Baroda Clocktower, by A.A. Raiba, 1997. Oil on canvas. Collection unknown. Photograph courtesy the artist.

Acknowledgements

I would like to thank Shivaji K. Panikkar and Ajay Sinha for their astute comments on this Introduction, and photographer Manish Chauhan for his willing cooperation.

For their help in the preparation of this volume, I would also like to thank:

H.H. Rajmata Shubhanginiraje Gaekwad, Chairperson, Maharaja Fatesingh Museum Trust, H.H. Maharaja Samarjitsinh Gaekwad and H.H. Maharani Radhikaraje Gaekwad.

Philippe Peycam and Willem Vogelsang of the International Institute for Asian Studies, Leiden.

Saranindranath Tagore, Andrea Pinkney, Maurizio Peleggi, Rahul Mukherji, Gyanesh Kudaisya, Frederick Asher, John Clark, Kamalika Bose, Giles Tillotson.

Rashmimala Devi, Christopher W. London, Gulammohammed and Nilima Sheikh for assisting with photo research.

Parul Dave Mukherji, Sandhya Bordewekar-Gajjar, Chandramohan, Monisha Ahmed, Rashmi Poddar, Menaka Kumari Shah, Durriya Dohadwala, Poonam Chawla, Dr Bhanu Ranjan.

7
Chimnabai Clocktower, Raopura, 1896, built in the Indo-Saracenic style with funds collected by the citizens of Baroda in memory of Maharani Chimnabai (1864–85).

8
Sayaji Clocktower, Sayajigunj, 1920–21. Engineer: A.H. Coyle; Clockmaker: Ranchhodlal K. Luhar.

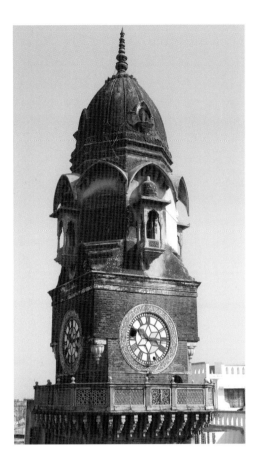

Jyoti Bhatt, Ratan Parimoo, Naina Dalal-Parimoo, B.V. Suresh, Indrapramit Roy, Vivan Sundaram, Vasudevan Akkitham, Rekha Rodwittiya, Surendran Nair, Pushpamala N., Nataraj Sharma, Kavita Shah, Vijay Bagodi, Nandini and Amitabh Gandhi, Krupa Amin, Ramchandra Gandhi, Sugata Ray, Atreyee Gupta.

Rahaab Allana of the Alkazi Collection of Photography, New Delhi.

Deepali Dewan and Nicola Wood of the Royal Ontario Museum.

Divia Patel and Anna Sheppard of the Victoria and Albert Museum, London.

K.K. Chakravarty of the Lalit Kala Akademi, New Delhi; Rajeev Lochan of the National Gallery of Modern Art, New Delhi; Dr A.N. Reddy of the Salar Jung Museum, Hyderabad; Manda Hingurao of the Maharaja Fatesingh Museum, Baroda; Oindrila Ray of the Tata Institute of Fundamental Research, Mumbai.

Mortimer Chatterjee, Tara Lal, Shireen Gandhy, Geetha Mehra, Sonia Ballaney.

H.G. Rathava, Chhaganbhai Solanki, G.J. Parmar, S.M. Patel, Manubhai Chauhan of the Gujarat State Archives, Southern Circle, Vadodara.

R.D. Parmar, Shailesh Ghoda, S.V. Patel, Rajendra Dhindorkar, Dr Dave of the Baroda Museum and Picture Gallery.

Hussain Ahmad Khan, COMSATS Institute of Information Technology, Lahore.

Murtaza Jafri, Rao Dilshad Ali, National College of Arts Archives, Lahore.

Notes

1   For further readings see, Partha Mitter, *The Triumph of Modernism: India's Artists and the Avant Garde: 1922–47*, London: Reaktion Books, 2007; Dipesh Chakrabarty, *Provincializing Europe:*

Postcolonial Thought and Historical Difference, Princeton and Oxford: Princeton University Press, 2000.

2   See the chapter by Shivaji Panikkar in this volume to understand this shift from a conventional/ pure art history which made descriptive, iconographic studies or region and chronology-based surveys, to the framing of a new art history along alternative and often political themes.

3   Sharada Dwivedi and Rahul Mehrotra, *Bombay: The Cities Within*, Mumbai: Eminence Designs, 2001; Giles Henry Rupert Tillotson, *Jaipur Nama: Tales from the Pink City*, New Delhi: Penguin Books, 2006; George Michell and Rana P.B. Singh, eds., *Banaras: The City Revealed*, Mumbai: Marg Publications, 2005; Neelum Saran Gour, ed., *Allahabad: Where the Rivers Meet*, Marg Publications, 2009.

The aforementioned books view their subject cities from very different vantage points though maintain their focus on the city's tangible/intangible heritage. Dwivedi and Mehrotra have the architecture of Bombay as their focal point of discussion, as well as their narrative tool to profile the city. Tillotson employs historical accounts of residents and travellers to interpret Jaipur's architecture, art and heritage. Theoretically he advances the idea of an indigenous art school which guides Jaipur's art and craft development, thereby debunking the widely perceived idea of referencing European art schools. Michell and Singh pay particular attention to the built forms and artistic achievements of Banaras against its political/dynastic and economic backdrops, chiefly Mauryan, pre-Sultanate, Sultanate, Mughal and British. Primarily the volume remains an investigation of architectural history. Gour's work reveals Allahabad's multiple contributions to the making of modern India: Hindi literature, Urdu and Persian poetry, law, architecture and art, political ideologies. This book on Baroda is situated in a wide sweep of both time and themes, and a slightly more alternative approach.

4   As we progressed on this volume, a seminal digitization project took shape – The Baroda Archives project, as part of the Asia Art Archive. Further references to the project are found in the chapter by Chithra K.S., Rashmimala Devi and Sabih Ahmed.

5   Dr Sunil Kothari, the noted writer and critic on Indian classical dance, points out the pioneering role of M.S. University in introducing courses in the performing arts. Kothari writes: "The most valuable contribution came in terms of Professor Mohan Khokhar who headed the Department of Classical Dance where two main streams were taught, Bharatanatyam and Kathak" (email dated March 2, 2015). Kothari himself was the first in India to complete a doctorate in dance, studying at M.S. University under Anjali Merh (who like Mohan Khokhar was from Kalakshetra). Baroda's contribution to music and dance is not within the scope of this book, but would provide enough material for a separate study.

6   Now the Maharaja Fatesingh Museum.

7   The tracks were transferred from the Palace grounds to Kamatibaug.

8   Conversations with Ratan Parimoo and Naina Dalal-Parimoo, December 2014–January 2015.

9   VadFest is named after the city's contemporary official name, Vadodara. However, this volume uses the city's erstwhile, more historical name Baroda, for reasons explained here: Bendapudi Subbarao constructs the etymological history of Baroda and its physical locations through archaeological and literary sources. The Baroda that we refer to saw human settlement as early as 1000 BCE. In terms of our information of names and their definite locations, Baroda began as a village at the beginning of the Common era with a few hamlets on the west bank of the Vishwamitri river. The settlement spread to the east side of the river and was known as Vadapadraka (Leaf of the Banyan Tree) by 600 CE (location: present-day Kothi and Medical College); it was a township

known as Ankottaka by the 8th century CE (location: present-day Akota). Both names were in use as Ankottaka was the administrative centre and Vadapadraka was the trade hub. The citadel of Baroda was constructed in the Sultanate era in the 16th century, and at this time the name "Baroda" comes into usage, as learnt from numerous travellers' accounts. In close succession the city witnessed Mughal rule, heavier traffic of European travellers and the British Residency. Baroda also enjoyed names such as Radiapura, Chandanavati (City of Sandalwood) and Viravati (Abode of Warriors) at different times. Bendapudi Subbarao, *Baroda Through the Ages: Being the Report of an Excavation conducted in the Baroda Area 1951–52*, M.S. University Archaeology Series No. 1, Baroda: Faculty of Fine Arts, M.S. University, 1953, pp. 5, 9–11, 15, 104–05, 126–27. Also see Govindbhai Desai and A.B. Clarke, *Gazetteer of the Baroda State, Volume II: Administration*, Bombay: Times Press, 1923.

The city was officially renamed Vadodara, a derivation of the medieval Vadapadraka, in 1974. Although today for official purposes the name Vadodara is used, the sphere of art, architectural and artisanal production continues to associate with "Baroda" since colonial times. "Baroda" appears in the colonial archival records, which this volume employs as a point of departure. M.S. University with which the fine arts community associates strongly was also founded when the city was still called "Baroda"; hence art-historical discussions, including this book, tend to use the historical name, Baroda. The VadFest becomes the first instance of an arts project that utilizes the name Vadodara in truncated form.

10 Atreyee Gupta, "For every one of them, there are ten of us", A Baroda Diary, May 9–14 2007; http://www.aaa.org.hk/Diaaalogue/Details/111, accessed January 1, 2015.

11 Shekhar Gupta, "Saving Indian Liberalism from its Left-Liberal Elite", *India Today*, December 15, 2014, pp. 20–21.

12 It must be noted that Gupta's seemingly oversimplified characterization is applied here to explain the current state of the art community vis-a-vis a majority viewing public. The author acknowledges that the political split in the art world itself has a complex history and deserves a more nuanced characterization than Gupta's dichotomous "Left and Right".

To explain the political leanings of the art community briefly: As such, the art community from the early 20th century has mostly been non-political or apolitical, save for singular projects of political art such as the one produced in the context of the Bengal Famine of 1942–43 under the Communist Party. The left orientations of the visual arts community are first seen in the Progressive Artists' Group (PAG), Bombay (1940s) alongside similar orientations in theatre, film etc. And the 1990s mark a key moment when the art community grouped together under SAHMAT to counter-respond to a growing rightwing movement. However, the decade of the 2000s and its more recent events, including the heterogeneous responses to VadFest, point to a growing political split within the art community; these phenomena deserve substantial theorizing. (Conversation with Shivaji Panikkar, Shireen Gandhy of Gallery Chemould, Mumbai, and artist Hema Upadhyay, January 2015).

13 See Aatish Taseer's novel, *The Way Things Were*, New Delhi: Picador India, 2014, for a discussion of distortions and revisions of cultural history through generally ill-equipped frameworks by those who aspire to a Hindu Renaissance.

Baroda as Provenance

Ajay Sinha

In art history, the treatment of a province (geographical and socio-political region) as provenance (a sphere of cultural practice) has long been a heuristic tool for the authentication of art works scattered in museums and collections around the world. In India, it has also been used to propose the agency of individual artists, partly to compensate for their anonymity in a pre-modern period. However, issues shift in modern and contemporary art, where artistic intentions are fully explicated in a system of art galleries, art criticism, exhibition and auction catalogues, as well as advocacy of living individual artists who archive and curate their own work. To describe the modern and contemporary art in Baroda as a matter of *provenance* thus means to trace a set of visual and cultural preoccupations beyond individual artists, stylistic choices and political intentions, to the princely state of Baroda. This volume is a step in that methodological direction.

Provenance must offer other challenges and possibilities in the area of art-making. For example, it must critique, instead of affirming, what Molly Aitken has called the "intelligence" of artists in a pre-modern pictorial tradition.[1] The critique promises an important intervention – it refocuses contemporary art's investments in political representation. In current art criticism, provinces of art-making merge to represent the nation, and "the double discourse of the national and the modern" becomes a premise through which art in India not only encounters the universalist narratives of modernism produced at art centres in the West but also represents itself as a local and indigenous practice.[2] The nation-figure does not disappear with the globalization of contemporary art. Rather, it is reconfigured as a gateway through which artists assemble from different parts of the world to thematize global art at international venues of biennales and art fairs.[3] At those venues, a remarkable twist re-stages the national-modern as "dialects" (and "accents") of global contemporary art.[4] Against these ahistorical movements of the national-modern, provenance helps build historical depth and material density into the interpretation of modern and contemporary art.

The "Princely Modern" in Baroda

The concept of "princely modernity" offers a good way to provincialize the national-modern in Baroda's art practice.[5] In 1949, the Faculty of Fine Arts (FFA) was established as an important part of a newly formed Maharaja Sayajirao University of Baroda, itself a result of a liberal vision taking shape in the princely state in the late 19th and early 20th centuries.[6] Under the Gaekwad Maharaja Sayajirao III (r. 1875–1939), Baroda was transformed from a military regime carved in the late 18th century by the Maratha Gaekwads in a political struggle involving the Mughal viceroy of Gujarat, the Peshwas of Poona and the British, to a progressive state of colonial India.[7] Key among Sayajirao's many initiatives was comprehensive educational reform. This included free education in the vernacular across Baroda state, and the founding of the Baroda College in affiliation with the Bombay University in 1882. The "Library Movement" led to the establishment of the Central Library in Baroda, a programme of education in the proper use of a library and a network of mobile libraries to cover remote localities where no permanent collection was available. In this volume, Priya Maholay-Jaradi mentions the school of arts and sciences, called Kalabhavan, which was established in 1890 to train the local rural artisans in the industrial arts. The Maharaja proposed the independent Baroda University in 1908 in response to Lord Curzon's University Act (1904), which would have given the Bombay University unprecedented control over the curriculum and governance of colleges affiliated to it, including those in Baroda.

Sayajirao's reforms resisted British institutions through what Manu Bhagavan calls "colonial mimicry", after Homi Bhabha.[8] The mimicry proved problematic for the British for two reasons. One, the reforms were initiated by a princely state over which the colonial administration only had indirect control. Second, their beneficiaries were the citizens of Baroda, whom the Maharaja wished to make equal if not superior to any in the British empire. Colonial mimicry turned to open rebellion when the free-thinking Maharaja became embroiled in a media scandal during the Delhi Durbar of 1911, where he appeared before King George V and Queen Mary in plain white clothes and carrying a walking stick (instead of wearing the princely regalia and the royal star), bowed to the King but not the Queen, and turned his back on them instead of stepping away from the royal presence to a designated distance before turning. For Bhagavan, the Maharaja's various liberal-progressive initiatives also add up to a defiant form of nationalism in the opening decades of the 20th century, when protest movements are fuelled by Mahatma Gandhi's launching of satyagraha from his ashram in nearby Ahmedabad.

I suggest, however, that the nationalistic effect of Sayajirao's reforms does not characterize the provenance of liberalism in his princely state, for which another sort of archaeology is needed. True, the Maharaja's "University Movement" was "British, *but not quite*".[9] It was informed by a vision of Enlightenment, based on liberal rationality, scientific knowledge and individual and social ethics that reached for models beyond British institutions, to the post-Civil War land-grant universities in America, and the modernization of Japan through imperial initiatives during the Meiji period. In the early decades of the 20th century, when a strong movement for indigenous education was taking institutional forms, as in the Gandhian vernacular Gujarat Vidyapith in Ahmedabad and emulated elsewhere, or in Rabindranath Tagore's experiment with a pre-modern gurukula (residential school) at Santiniketan, the Maharaja's 19th-century form of liberalism must have also seemed nationalistic, but not quite.[10] As the Maharaja balances his anachronistic reforms with contemporary politics, Bhagavan notices a hint of pragmaticism in his delicate approach.[11]

Let me characterize princely modernity by exploring that pragmaticism in an anecdote from Baroda's visual culture. In the 1890s, before he became the father of Indian cinema, Dadasaheb Phalke established a career as a photographer and a magician in the princely state. As a fresh graduate from the newly established Kalabhavan in Baroda, Phalke's attempts at photography came up against a widespread belief that a photograph shortens the subject's life. His breakthrough came when he persuaded a prince (this may or may not have been Sayajirao III), who believed he was possessed by a ghost, that the camera

1
Baroda College (1880–82), which became the Maharaja Sayajirao University in 1949. Architects: Sir William Emerson, PRIBA and Robert F. Chisholm.

could cure his affliction. Phalke loaded up his camera with a negative on which he had sketched in advance a distorted figure, and asked the prince to pose for his photograph under a Pipal tree (frequently believed to be haunted by ghosts). The resulting negative impressed the prince so much that he went on to become a fervent advocate of that modern technology of vision and control.[12]

There are at least two ways of looking at this anecdote, one privileging the artist as a national figure, the other the provenance of the prince's response. Phalke's photographic trickery was a forerunner of his breakthrough in Indian cinema, where he made gods come alive on the movie screen.[13] But let us explore the provincial response to photography by asking, What exactly did the Maharaja see? At a literal level, we could say that he saw a scientific and mechanical procedure displayed as a means of transcendence, making the ghosts of the past disappear under his very eyes. But we could also say the opposite – namely, that the Maharaja became an advocate of photography precisely after seeing in that transcendent technology a clear (if ghostly!) figuration of his pre- or extra-modern past. His rational-liberal interests may then follow from this reflective possibility in the modern scientific and industrial medium.[14]

Mimesis of a global technology, not mimicry of local politics, is at issue in this pragmaticism. In this volume, scholars investigate Baroda's art and culture within an expansive framework of global modernity, using "cosmopolitanism" to reflect better the diverse set of global references in the art, architecture, museological and archival practices in Baroda.[15] Of course, Baroda will need to be distinguished from other provinces so that cosmopolitanism does not become one more means to re-cast the national modern by merging provinces of art.[16]

In the volume, Priya Maholay-Jaradi explains Baroda's pragmaticism in Maharaja Sayajirao's patronage of what she calls "the new aesthetic of Indian design". "Design" was a novel idea for organizing artistic labour to make goods that would compete in a global market. It was formulated in mid-18th-century London by the Department of Science and Art under Henry Cole; it was seen widely at mechanized workshops and factories in Europe and applied in 1890 at Kalabhavan, Baroda's institute of arts and sciences.[17] Design reimagined traditional artisanal practice within an art school curriculum by introducing drawing as a scientific means for measuring and accurately transferring shapes and decorative motifs from two-dimensional models to three-dimensional objects. Art school training also included a work ethic so that, under a "designer" at a manufacturing firm, artisans could organize themselves in an orderly group for producing standardized merchandise in some combination of handwork and machinery set up at factories. The Maharaja also collected such designed objects, gifting and lending them for colonial and international expositions.

A vivid example of the new ethic and aesthetic of Indian design is a silver tea service the Maharaja gifted to the Prince of Wales, Prince Albert Edward (later Edward VII), during his visit to India in the winter of 1875–76. The set was made by the Scottish design and manufacturing firm P. Orr & Sons in Madras, and called Swami silver because of the depiction of Hindu gods on its individual pieces. The Maharaja intended the tea service as a gift to symbolize his allegiance to the English Crown within a new imperial diplomacy that came into existence after the insurgency of 1857. It indicated his cosmopolitanism in two ways. One, it followed the ethical standards of British industry, as attested by a photo album of P. Orr & Sons from 1899, one image showing factory spaces with workers at rows of tables working with hand and machinery under clocks, and another of the firm's Madras showroom

2

Design of the silver teapot, from the tea service manufactured by P. Orr & Sons, Madras, gifted by Maharaja Sayajirao III to the Prince of Wales in 1875–76. From P. Orr & Sons, Swami Catalogue of 1877.

fitted like a fine arts gallery, with glass and mirror showcases filled with silverware. Incidentally, the showroom was designed by R.F. Chisholm, the well-known Madras architect and the principal of the Madras School of Art, who also designed the Lakshmi Vilas Palace in Baroda. According to Dipti Khera, the firm of P. Orr & Sons presented a "modernizing narrative" for artisans and manufacture, distinguishing them from "native craftsmen" who sold an array of goods at chaotic Oriental bazaars, representing India's backwardness to a metropolitan imagination.[18] Second, as Khera also demonstrates, the illustrations for the Swami silver in the firm's sales catalogues were based on Edward Moor's *Hindu Pantheon* (1810), a classic introduction providing correct, scientific and ethnographic knowledge of gods in Hindu art, aimed at dispelling their reputation as monstrosities, a common misconception at the time among European archaeologists, antiquarians, administrators and travellers in India. Moreover, accompanying the Gaekwad set was a booklet titled *Hindoo Mythology Popularly Treated: Being an Epitomized Description of the Various Heathen Deities Illustrated on the Silver Swami Tea Service, by His Highness Gaekwar of Baroda*, apparently intended as an instructional guide for Prince Edward.[19]

The set was prominently featured in the Paris Exposition Universelle of 1878, where, however, it was seen to exemplify cosmopolitanism of the wrong sort. George C.M. Birdwood, in his handbook for the Paris Exposition,[20] remarked: "Nothing could be worse than the tea tray and tea pot, and sugar and milk bowls, in this Madras tea service ... a monstrous product of the attempt to combine Indian with European designs in decorative arts."[21]

While disturbing colonial and nationalistic expectations in the late 19th and early 20th centuries, the mimesis of a rational-liberal ethic and aesthetic described so far suggests a princely variant of cosmopolitanism on which the visual culture of Baroda is premised.[22] How does Baroda's late-20th-century art reflect this princely modern provenance of cosmopolitanism?

Role of the Faculty of Fine Arts

In 1949, when the M.S. University of Baroda finally took ground, the FFA was made its centrepiece. Describing its mission, Hansa Mehta, the university's first Vice Chancellor and the daughter of Dewan Manubhai Mehta who had drafted the most comprehensive report for the possible university in 1927, wrote: "The education that a student receives in this Faculty is of a varied nature combining both theory and practice of art. The courses also provide a liberal education that would enable students to appreciate art better."[23] As Nilima Sheikh explains, Mehta's idea of the artist differed from other contemporary models, such as that of a traditional, village artisan imagined in Tagore's Santiniketan, and the modernist image of a free-thinking social rebel imagined by the Progressive Artists' Group in Bombay. In Mehta's vision, there was a new alignment of skills and learning. Baroda's diversified curriculum took from the post-Bauhaus methodology of American art schools that trained students to deduce design principles from a visual perception of the everyday. Naturalistic drawing aimed to exploit different kinds of materials, beyond the mastery of academic categories of portraiture, life-study, landscape etc. that informed the curricula of colonial institutions such as the Sir J.J. School of Art in Bombay. World art history was made an integral part of the programme to allow students to locate their practical courses

3
View of Watchroom at P. Orr & Sons,
Mount Road, Madras. Unknown
photographer, c. 1891. Albumen print
mounted on album page, 33 x 82 cm.
Courtesy of the Royal Ontario Museum,
© ROM. Accession No. 2006.95.1.8 –
this acquisition was made possible by the
generous support of the Louise Hawley
Stone Charitable Trust.

4
View of principal showroom at P. Orr &
Sons, Mount Road, Madras. Unknown
photographer, c. 1891. Albumen print
mounted on album page, 33 x 82 cm.
Courtesy of the Royal Ontario Museum,
© ROM. Accession No. 2006.95.1.4 –
this acquisition was made possible by the
generous support of the Louise Hawley
Stone Charitable Trust.

in a global context.[24] The diversity was founded on the "princely modern" provenance of pragmaticism, which is remarkable also because it steers clear from any ideological affiliation with strands of nationalism informing art training in the decades around Independence.[25]

Many essays in this volume explore the influence of the FFA on Baroda's practising artists. Ratan Parimoo's account of N.S. Bendre, who developed Baroda's painting curriculum in the 1950s, is a significant example of the princely provenance of modernism. An artist trained in the princely state of Indore, Bendre inspired many artists in Baroda as well as in Bombay. Parimoo describes Bendre's virtuoso mastery of various modernist styles, which he freely displayed in his gouache and encaustic works, as well as in class demonstrations he staged for his mesmerized students. Bendre's art and pedagogy transform modernism into an artisanal practice, making modernist styles available as a shared resource for students, while also dismantling modernism's preoccupation with artistic individuality. Parimoo, a student fresh from Kashmir in the 1950s, defines Bendre's modernism as "Indian". But the term has a different ring than the ideological production of "Indian" modern art in Bengal, which was an explicit critique of British notions of native crafts, waged by elite Indian nationalists and European Orientalists in Calcutta.[26] By contrast, Bendre opened up possibilities for students to imagine themselves as self-declared artists and designers in post-Independence textile and advertising industries, continuing the spirit of liberal education at the centre of the university.[27]

Karin Zitzewitz discusses the career of Bendre's student, Jyoti Bhatt, as a printmaker, designer and photographer. The Baroda provenance of Bhatt's work is visible in his photography of rural Gujarat and Rajasthan. Bhatt draws his attachment to rural Gujarat from his early schooling at a Gandhian institution, Shri Dakshinamurti Vidyarthi Bhavan in Bhavnagar. But, remarkably, Bhatt differs from the nationalist fervour of his mentor, Ravishankar Raval (1892–1977), another Bhavnagari who brings his experience as a journalist, writer and artist to bear on what Ratan Parimoo has described as a Gandhian renaissance.[28] Raval becomes involved in Gandhi's Swadeshi movement after settling in Ahmedabad in 1919, and defines an indigenous art practice by turning to the revivalist art of Bengal, the Rajput School of miniature paintings and Ajanta murals. By contrast, Bhatt poses village women in their embroidered clothes against the elaborate, maze-like patterns made with rice flour on the floors and mud walls of their huts, setting up a metonymic relationship between the figure and the ground. Zitzewitz relates Bhatt's formal wit to the French photographer, Henri Cartier-Bresson. Beyond the artist's cosmopolitan sensibility, however, Bhatt's photographs are obsessed with the magic and mystery of Gujarat's rural lands, to which he returns repeatedly. His images are possessed by what Walter Benjamin might call the rural landscape's "optical unconscious",[29] revealed by photography in a way similar to Phalke's "trickery" in an earlier era at Baroda.

Closing Thoughts
Manu Bhagavan best describes Baroda's princely modern culture as "possession of the modern", suggesting an enchantment with the gaze of modernity that arrives in India through colonialism.[30] In 1908, Sayajirao predicted that modernity would inevitably lead to a future where the "Princely Order" would disappear.[31] Bhagavan hears a nationalistic spirit in that radical claim, but in the early decades of the 20th century, when nationalism was becoming militant through Gandhi's sharp distinction between passive resistance and the stronger form of "civil disobedience" he called satyagraha, the Maharaja's brand of

5
Sketch of Lakshmi Vilas Palace, by
Ranjitsinh Gaekwad, 1994. Ink on paper,
56 x 76 cm. Collection: Late Maharaja
Ranjitsinh Gaekwad.

nationalism would have appeared too passive.[32] In it, we only find a tactical recognition of the inevitable change modernity would bring about, in which he imagined liberalism as a means for shaping a plebeian vision for his princely state.

An ink drawing by Ranjitsinh Gaekwad, a graduate of the FFA, made in 1994 when he held the defunct title of Maharaja of Baroda, offers a suggestive image of the plebeian vision at the core of the Baroda provenance of visual culture. The drawing shows a fragmented, low-angle view of domes and turrets of the Lakshmi Vilas Palace. The image is striking because it is not a record of ownership comparable to, say, a painting of 18th-century English country estates by the painter Thomas Gainsborough, or typical 19th-century photographic views of the Palace, or similar renditions by the Hungarian artists Sass and Elizabeth Brunner, who sojourned in Baroda in the late 1930s. Nor is it a Gandhian icon. The partial view of the half-obscured exterior, crumbling into dotted compositional lines and palm foliage at the bottom of the page, makes the gorgeous Palace seem no more than an ordinary landmark in the city, similar to the Baroda train station, the Nyaya Mandir or the Museum and Picture Gallery in Kamatibaug across from the college, with which students regularly fill their sketchbooks. Readers will benefit from reading "across" the essays in this volume to similarly discover the coordinates of Baroda's provenance in the deep, diachronic history of visual culture that threads through them.

Notes

1   Molly Emma Aitken, *The Intelligence of Tradition in Rajput Court Painting*, New Haven: Yale University Press, 2010.

2   Geeta Kapur, *When Was Modernism: Essays in Contemporary Cultural Practice in India*, New Delhi: Tulika, 2000, p. 288.

6
Painting of Lakshmi Vilas Palace, by Sass Brunner, 1938. Oil on canvas. Courtesy of the Department of Museums, Museum and Picture Gallery, Baroda. Not to be reproduced without prior permission of the Director of Museums.

3   See Terry Smith, "Introduction: The Contemporaneity Question", in Terry Smith, Okwui Enwezor and Nancy Condee, eds., *Antinomies of Art and Culture: Modernity, Postmodernity, and Contemporaneity*, Durham, North Carolina: Duke University Press, 2008.

4   Juliana Engberg, artistic director of the 2014 Biennale of Sydney and Artistic Director of the Australian Centre of Contemporary Art, Sydney, in "Conversations: The Global Art World, Making Biennales", Art BaselOnline Video Archive, Hong Kong, 2014, at artbasel.com (accessed July 15, 2014).

5   Manu Bhagavan, *Sovereign Spheres: Princes, Education and Empire in Colonial India*, Delhi: Oxford University Press, 2003, p. 5.

6   Manu Bhagavan, "The Rebel Academy: Modernity and the Movement for a University in Princely Baroda, 1908–49", *The Journal of Asian Studies*, Vol. 61, No. 3, August 2002, pp. 919–47.

7   David Hardiman, "Baroda: The Structure of a 'Progressive' State", in Robin Jeffrey, ed., *People, Princes and Paramount Power*, Delhi: Oxford University Press, 1978, pp. 107–35.

8   Bhagavan, 2002, pp. 921–22.

9   Ibid.

10 Bhagavan's idea of "princely modernity" is effectively applied to progressive thought and education in the court of Tanjore/Thanjavur in the 1800s, before the question of colonial resistance occurs. See Indira Viswanathan Peterson, "The Schools of Serfoji II of Tanjore: Education and Princely Modernity in Early Nineteenth-century India", in Michael S. Dodson and Brian A. Hatcher, eds., *Trans-Colonial Modernities in South Asia*, London and New York: Routledge, 2012, pp. 15–44. The genealogy of Baroda's princely modernity could partly be traced to Tanjore, hometown of Sayajirao's first visionary Dewan and regent, T. Madhava Rao, as well as Sayajirao's first wife, Maharani Chimnabai I.

11 Bhagavan, 2003, p. 69.

12 Isak Mujawar, *Dadasaheb Phalke* (Marathi), Pune: Sadhana Prakashan, 1970, pp. 10–11. It is unclear from the biography whether the prince, called "Maharaja" as well as a "sansthanik" (an official), was indeed Sayajirao Gaekwad.

13 Christopher Pinney, *Camera Indica: The Social Life of Indian Photographs,* Chicago: University of Chicago Press, 1997, pp. 92–93.

14 The Maharaja is not known to have taken up photography himself, unlike, say, Maharaja Ram Singh II of Jaipur. Nor did he overcome his ghosts, if we go by another anecdote from the early 20th century relating to an insurgent peasant leader, Daduram. Apparently, the leader was imprisoned by Sayajirao in 1907. But when the Maharaja went to meet him in prison, Daduram used magical (could it be photographical?) powers to multiply himself, which made his captor fall to his knees in reverence to what he believed to be a divine presence. See Vinayak Chaturvedi, *Peasant Pasts: Histories and Memories in Western India*, Berkeley, Los Angeles and London: University of California Press, 2007, pp. 174–75.

15 See also Julie F. Codell, "Ironies of Mimicry: The Art Collection of Sayaji Rao III Gaekwad, Maharaja of Baroda, and the Cultural Politics of Early-Modern India", *Journal of the History of Collections*, Vol. 15, No. 1, 2003, pp. 127–46.

16 Pragmaticism might help distinguish Baroda, for instance, from what Partha Mitter identifies as a "virtual cosmopolis" in Calcutta during the late 19th and early 20th centuries, when elite bhadralok produced an intellectual renaissance of Bengali art and literature. Partha Mitter, "Decentering Modernism: Art History and Avant Garde Art from the Periphery", *Art Bulletin*, Vol. XC, No. 4, December 2008, p. 542. Also see Partha Mitter, *The Triumph of Modernism: India's Artists and the Avant-garde, 1922–1947,* New Delhi and New York: Oxford University Press, 2007, for a full elaboration of the idea.

17 Arindam Dutta, *The Bureaucracy of Beauty: Design in the Age of its Global Reproducibility*, New York: Routledge, 2006. Also Makarand Mehta, "Science versus Technology: The Early Years of the Kala Bhavan, Baroda, 1890–1896", *Indian Journal of History of Science*, Vol. 27, No. 2, 1992, pp. 145–70.

18 Dipti Khera, "'Designs to Suit Every Taste': P. Orr & Sons and *Swami* Silverware", in Vidya Dehejia, ed., *Delight in Design: Indian Silver for the Raj*, Ahmedabad: Mapin Publishing, 2008, pp. 20–37 (see pp. 26–29).

19 Ibid., p. 24.

20 George C.M. Birdwood, *Paris Universal Exhibition of 1878: Hand Book to the British Section, Presentation Edition,* London and Paris: Offices of the Royal Commission, 1878. Later editions for wider circulation were titled *The Industrial Arts of India*, London: Chapman and Hall Limited, 1880.

21 Birdwood, 1878, pp. 60 and 72, quoted in Khera, 2008, p. 22.

22 See also Maholay-Jaradi's discussion of Raja Ravi Varma in this volume. The "trans-colonial" promise of modernity tends to be reduced to "colonial mimicry" or "colonial resistance", skewing Baroda's "princely" provenance towards what C.A. Bayly calls a "post-colonial cringe". C.A. Bayly, "Afterword: Bombay's 'Intertwined Modernities', 1780–1880," in Dodson and Hatcher, eds., *Trans-Colonial Modernities in South Asia*, 2012, p. 237.

23 Brochure dated 1953, quoted in Nilima Sheikh, "A Post-Independence Initiative in Art", in Gulammohammed Sheikh, ed., *Contemporary Art in Baroda*, New Delhi: Tulika, 1997, p. 55.

24 Ibid., pp. 55–56.

25 This stance of Baroda's Fine Arts curriculum maps nicely with David Hardiman's analysis of Baroda's ambiguous relationship to Gandhi's satyagraha among peasants in British Gujarat, and

also Baroda's reluctance in becoming part of the newly formed Bombay state at Independence. Hardiman, 1978, esp. pp. 129–31.

26 Tapati Guha-Thakurta, "Orientalism and the New Claims for Indian Art", in *The Making of a New "Indian" Art: Artists, Aesthetics, and Nationalism in Bengal, c. 1850–1920*, Cambridge (England) and New York: Cambridge University Press, 1992, pp. 146–84.

27 Nilima Sheikh, 1997. Bendre's artisanal approach to modernism must be distinguished from the primitivism informing Santiniketan's pedagogy or the art of Jamini Roy. For the latter, see Mitter, *The Triumph of Modernism,* 2007. Bendre might be better seen in relation to what we might call Indore Modernism, where Maharaja Yeshwantrao Holkar II (r. 1926–61) was famously invested in European modernist trends. His Manikbaug Palace was designed in 1930–32 by Eckart Muthesius, a designer of strong modernist sensibility, whom he met in Oxford. The fully air-conditioned palace included furniture designed by German and French designers. The Maharaja owned two marble sculptures of Constantin Brancusi, who also visited Indore in 1937 to plan an open-air temple that, however, was never realized. See Amin Jaffer, *Made for Maharajas: A Design Diary of Princely India*, New York: The Vendome Press, 2007, p. 269; also see p. 96, for a photograph of the dapper Maharaja by the surrealist photographer Man Ray, who visited the Maharaja and his wife in Cannes in 1930 and with whom they shared a passion for jazz.

28 Ratan Parimoo, "Ravishankar Raval Initiates Renaissance of Art in Gujarat", in Ratan Parimoo and Sandip Sarkar, eds., *Historical Development of Contemporary Indian Art, 1880–1947*, New Delhi: Lalit Kala Akademi, 2009, pp. 295–313.

29 Walter Benjamin, "The Work of Art in the Age of Its Technological Reproducibility", second version, in Michael W. Jennings, Brigid Doherty and Thomas Y. Levin, eds., *Walter Benjamin: The Work of Art in the Age of Its Technological Reproducibility and Other Writings on Media*, Cambridge, Mass., and London, England, The Belknap Press of Harvard University Press, 2008, p. 37.

30 "It was the possession of the modern by the native that changed the course of the concept into the very opposite of that prescribed by British promoters of such policy, that is people who believed that modern institutions were instruments of colonialism." Manu Bhagavan, "Demystifying the 'Ideal Progressive': Resistance through Mimicked Modernity in Princely Baroda, 1900–1913", *Modern Asian Studies*, Vol. 35, No. 2, May 2001, p. 409.

31 "British rule in India … will never be ended merely by the struggle of the Indian people. But world conditions are bound to change so fundamentally that nothing will then be able to prevent its total disappearance …. The first thing you'll have to do when the English are gone is to get rid of all these rubbishy states. I tell you, there'll never be an Indian nation until this so-called Princely Order disappears." A conversation between the Maharaja and the Aga Khan, quoted in Bhagavan, 2001, p. 394. The Maharaja's idea of princely states as colonial puppets refers to Lord Dalhousie's aggressive means in the mid-19th century of imposing indirect rule of the East India Company over the princely states.

32 See the distinction made in M.K. Gandhi, "Letter to Mr. ——", January 25, 1920, *The Collected Works of Mahatma Gandhi*, New Delhi: Ministry of Information and Broadcasting, 2000, Vol. 19, p. 350.

"Baroda" at Colonial Exhibitions (1878–1904)

Priya Maholay-Jaradi

PERFORATED BETEL BOX.   ROSE WATER SPRINKLER.   LOTAH.
SILVER WORK. BARODA.

George Birdwood's foundational survey of Indian crafts for the Paris Universal Exhibition of 1878, which became widely circulated as *The Industrial Arts of India*, the handbook for the Paris Exposition, 1880, attributes five entries to Baroda: two craft genres and three royal objects.[1] Two and a half decades later, George Watt's catalogue of the Delhi Durbar Exhibition, 1904, documents 13 crafts and seven royal objects as representative of Baroda.[2] Unlike Birdwood's catalogue, the 1904 documentation gives extended entries for each genre with details of technique, medium, motifs and popular practitioners. How does Baroda negotiate this journey from 1880 to 1904 to emerge as an independent provenance with such extensive representation? An examination of the Baroda Durbar's loans to colonial exhibitions helps one understand how the Maharaja and his officers constructed a representative category of Baroda arts and crafts.

The Emergence of a Provenance

The Colonial and Indian Exhibition in London, 1886, made a marked shift from national pavilions to provincial courts for display.[3] Few craft genres were exclusive to Baroda, and the Maharaja's office recorded fewer artisans in the state when compared to Ahmedabad and Surat.[4] As a result, Baroda participated as a section of the Bombay Court.[5] From here on, it becomes crucial to note the repeated display of exclusive genres and the inclusion of new ones from surveys, polytechnics, workshops and the royal palace to create an independent Baroda Court. This not only evidences a strategy to meet reasonable numbers, but also shows how each segment was driven by distinct ideas, which converged to create a cosmopolitan space.

The 1886 loans' inventory records 772 articles loaned by Baroda state.[6] I discern the following groups:

- Traditional crafts: Patan pottery, Bilimora ivory inlay work, sandalwood work, bison horn products, Visnagar brassware, Dabhoi and Kadi brass and copperware;
- Objects of royal consumption: jewellery and textiles lent by the Durbar as well as purchased;
- Royal pageantry items: silver model of a state elephant, silver bullock carriage, silver dumni (palanquin); photographs of actual state processions;
- Ethnological collection: plaster models of ethnic types;
- Special commissions: Baroda Screen, Baroda Balcony, Pigeon House;

- Miscellaneous: marble knick-knacks, gold and silver thread embroidery; calico printing, fabrics and weaves.[7]

Next, we move to the Chicago World's Fair, 1893. Despite the Fair's display being organized along ethnological categories,[8] the Baroda Durbar persisted with the original proposition to be represented as an independent court.[9] Clearly, the Durbar had come a long way since its 1886 lament of few artisans and exclusive genres. Its loan inventory had expanded and its loan policy was revised considerably. An examination of the 1893 Baroda loan demonstrates the continued presence of well-received genres from the 1886 loan as well as ongoing experiments in private patronage and institutional projects undertaken by the Maharaja. One sees the continued presence of pageantry items, gold and silver jewels and traditional crafts from Patan, Bilimora and Kadi; among the new additions, Baroda's polytechnic Kalabhavan makes a distinct debut with lacquerware, furniture and woodwork; in the domain of the high arts, the small loans of two or three genre paintings seen previously at the 1879 Simla Fine Arts Exhibition and subsequent exhibitions in Poona now mature into a series of ten paintings of Indian women by Raja Ravi Varma.[10]

The above inventories see the integration of three sites: the traditional, industrial and the royal, which correspond to the products of artisans/craftspeople, polytechnics/ workshops and the royal palace. Quite simply put, for Baroda's loans, the explanation of cosmopolitanism as an attitude of openness suffices.[11] "The political philosophy of cosmopolitanism has always upheld the spirit of openness and a perspective on the world that emphasized the extension of the bonds of inclusivity."[12] Going by this explanation, cosmopolitanism is a condition which is in opposition with prevalent conditions and thus seeks alternatives to the existing state of affairs.[13]

One applies the idea of opposition with the status quo to the dichotomy between superior, European, machine-produced goods, and aesthetic hand-produced Indian crafts. This set the direction for all art-craft appraisals from the Great Exhibition of 1851 onward.[14] The status quo was challenged by Sayajirao through a systematic cultivation of ideas which guided his private patronage as well as institutional projects. The crux of these ideas was that, despite colonialism, India could have its own unique genres of art and craft; moreover their production could rely on native practices as well as (perceived) universal standards, such as mechanization.[15] This point helps to frame the case-study of Sayajirao and Baroda state's loans to exhibitions within the genre of aesthetic cosmopolitanism, which is premised on two main conditions: one being that a cosmopolitical worldview can be produced through aesthetics; the second being the cultural condition in which local modes of production and consumption dialogue with globally hegemonic forms and networks.[16] While aesthetic cosmopolitanism has been conceived in the realm of contemporary arts and globalization, here the idea is relocated in the colonial encounter of globalization. Just as cosmopolitan tendencies in contemporary art are not a result of globalization, so also European-style art practices alongside native conventions cannot be read as mere manifestations of the colonial-global encounter. Instead, as mentioned earlier, Sayajirao's ideas and imagination as a patron, coupled with reason and strategy in his role as head of state, alter the status quo – as will be revealed below in the discussion of singular projects undertaken by the Maharaja in Baroda state.

1
Perforated betel box, rosewater sprinkler and lota, examples of Baroda silverwork. Colour plate reproduced from B.A. Gupte, "The Baroda Court", *Journal of Indian Art and Industry,* London: W. Griggs, 1886. The plates are not numbered but placed after the article, pp. 126–33. Courtesy of the National College of Arts Archives, Lahore.

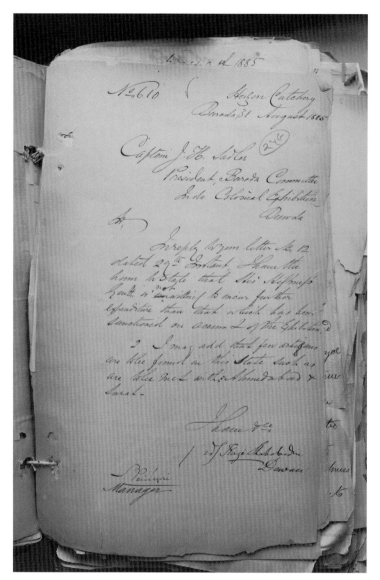

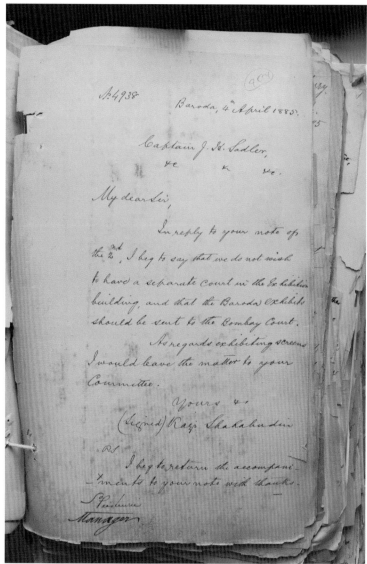

Traditional Crafts and State Surveys

Sayajirao's mentor and Dewan of Baroda state (1875–82), T. Madhava Rao, actively supported craftsmen at the royal palace of Baroda, Lakshmi Vilas.[17] These craftsmen, working in ivory and mica, were not native to Baroda but the Durbar loaned their works to the Poona Fine Arts Exhibition, 1878 and the Simla Fine Arts Exhibition, 1879.[18] Alongside engagement with artisans from outside Baroda, Madhava Rao sourced and loaned local craft samples such as Baroda lace and embroidery.[19] Native genres such as pottery and their caste-based artisans were placed within the context of workshops to avail of new materials, techniques and experiments.[20]

Drawing up a crafts' inventory continued actively under Sayajirao's tenure. His statewide tours culminated in a documentation of local crafts in a volume dedicated to Baroda in the 1883 Gazetteer of Bombay.[21] Thus, employment of artisans at the royal palace as well as statewide surveys culminated in the first few loans' inventories from as early as 1878. Though Sayajirao's direct agency may not be seen in each of the above examples, the shared context of his roles as royal patron, head of state and lender facilitates the agency of his

2
Letter 610 from Huzur Cutchery (Sayajirao's office) lamenting fewer artisans in Baroda as compared to Ahmedabad and Surat. Collection: Gujarat State Archives, Southern Circle, Vadodara, Huzur Political Office.

3
Letter 4938 from Huzur Cutchery (Sayajirao's office) proposing Baroda's participation as part of the Bombay Court at the 1886 Exhibition. Collection: Gujarat State Archives, Southern Circle, Vadodara, Huzur Political Office.

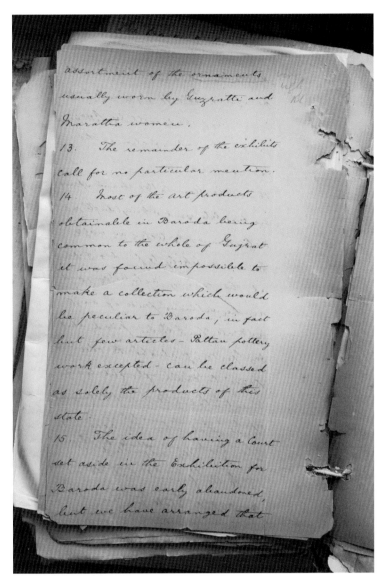

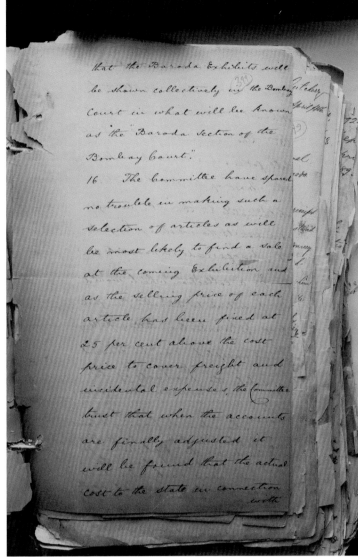

4 & 5
Two pages from Letter 34 from Huzur Cutchery (Sayajirao's office) expressing the impossibility of building a collection peculiar to Baroda and hence supporting Baroda's participation as part of the Bombay Court at the 1886 Exhibition. Collection: Gujarat State Archives, Southern Circle, Vadodara, Huzur Political Office.

resource persons and links up royal commissions and statewide projects with exhibitions. Consequently the space of patronage and loans displays openness to diverse artistic traditions.

Kalabhavan

Sayajirao acknowledged that the viability of Indian crafts could not rest on aesthetic competency alone. These genres had to be competent economically and qualitatively in global markets. He supported the idea that while handiwork cannot replace all industry, it can be bettered with new techniques of production. In his speech at the Ahmedabad Industrial Exhibition, 1902, Sayajirao suggested "… the true remedy for any old industry which needs support is to study the market, find out what is wanted and improve the finish of the work and the design until an increasing demand shows that the right direction has been found. This applies particularly to the artistic trades, such as wood-carving and metal-work, for which the country has been so famous and which it would be a pity to allow to die altogether."[22] Placing Sayajirao's speeches alongside his projects demonstrates how his normative dispositions translate into empirical work.[23]

In keeping with his idea about the improvement of craft production, Sayajirao established Baroda's premier polytechnic, Kalabhavan in 1890.[24] Its curriculum reflects the inclusion of artisanal, mechanical, technical and art school disciplines. The founder-principal, T.K. Gajjar, undertook extensive tours of the state to understand traditional industries such as dyeing, printing and woodwork which were reflected in the curriculum.[25] The staff included professors and laboratory assistants alongside caste-based artisans.[26] Additionally, Kalabhavan utilized a workshop with extensive machinery for the practical training of its students.[27]

Given the Maharaja's position as patron and head of state, Kalabhavan regularly produced items for exhibition loans,[28] making its debut in 1893 at Chicago. The regular inclusion of the polytechnic's products in Baroda's loans, made them representative of the state's arts and crafts; to the extent that Baroda proposed an independent edition of the Ahmedabad Industrial Exhibition in 1902–03 on the strength of Kalabhavan products.[29] One of the old objections against cosmopolitanism is that it fails to engage the local and remains a

6
Kalabhavan (now Senapati Bhavan). From *Views of Palaces and Places of Interest in Baroda*, by V.G. Chiplonkar, active 1900s. Gelatin silver print, c. 1903. The Alkazi Collection of Photography.

7
"His Highness Maharaja Sayaji-Rav, Gaikwar." Colour plate reproduced from B.A. Gupte, "The Baroda Court", *Journal of Indian Art and Industry*, London: W. Griggs, 1886. Courtesy of the National College of Arts Archives, Lahore.

global ideology which embraces the world of the mobile global elite.[30] The Kalabhavan experiment demonstrates how Sayajirao's cosmopolitanism was not merely confined to local or global ideologies but instead included rural and urban artisans alongside fine artists in locally relevant projects.

Indian and Vernacular Design
The Maharaja's art patronage also supported the loan of Indian design to international exhibitions and firms. As seen earlier, Indian design had been received as a superior aesthetic since 1851 (the year of the Great Exhibition in London) and became much sought after, being applied to enhance the otherwise uniform, mass-produced British goods.[31] Within this context of a growing taste for Indian design, maharajas commissioned luxury goods which were Indian or European in form and Indian in design.[32] In addition to objects of personal use such as jewellery and toiletries, gift articles such as tea sets were custom-made. One such tea set was gifted by Sayajirao to the Prince of Wales in 1875–76 and later displayed at the Paris Universal Exhibition, 1878.[33] Evidently, the royal patron's socio-economic status plugged Indian design on the international circuit of gift exchange, display and taste-making. The design for this tea set incorporated a contemporary reconfiguration of Swamis or Hindu gods, a signature experiment by the Madras-based P. Orr & Sons.[34] Lakshmi Vilas, with its extensive treasures of jewels and paraphernalia also became a design archive which was referenced to create new items. Architect Charles Mant likely referred to royal jewels for designing a walking stick, again commissioned to P. Orr & Sons, Madras.[35]

The courting of Indian design by the cosmopolitan ethos of machine-produced goods raises the question: Was mechanization the sole standard for production? This new aesthetic of Indian design, promoted by patrons such as Sayajirao, became an *alternative standard*, thereby debunking the myth of the universal. The provincial rose to the level of the universal as Europe co-opted components of other non-European world cultures to strengthen its own industrial experiments. This also sheds light on the mutually constitutive nature of the vernacular and cosmopolitan.[36] The tea set and walking stick, examples of generic Indian design, prove how Indian design's native affiliation was often exchanged for a more international affiliation with metropolitan markets. Thus lending agencies such as P. Orr & Sons and the Lakshmi Vilas Palace became de-provincialized in the global space of commercial markets. In stark contrast, at exhibitions, Indian design was increasingly classified, labelled and provincialized – as I explore next.

Exhibitions ferreted out local artisanal designs which were replicated on large-scale gateways, balconies and screens. This experiment is best illustrated in the Baroda Screen, produced jointly by native artisans from Patan district in Baroda and Mr Wimbridge of the East India Art Manufacturing Company for the 1886 Exhibition; details of the design were taken from houses in neighbouring Surat.[37] Despite being a part of the Bombay Court in 1886, Baroda was comprehensively documented and lavishly illustrated in the *Journal of Indian Art and Industry*.[38] This explains why the "Baroda provenance" lasted beyond the ephemera of exhibitions. The practice of classification, labelling, nomenclature and comprehensive cataloguing became entrenched in colonial exhibitions.[39] Frequent lender-states enjoyed repeated visibility through new catalogues and gradually became established as centres of patronage and/or production.

GOLD AND SILK BROCADE.

GOLD EMBROIDERED JACKET.

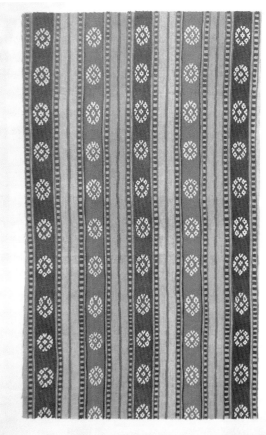

SATIN. *MASHRU.*

EXHIBITED BY THE BARODA COMMITTEE.

PRINTED *SADI.*

EXHIBITED BY THE BARODA COMMITTEE.

8–10
Colour plates reproduced from B.A. Gupte, "The Baroda Court", *Journal of Indian Art and Industry*, London: W. Griggs, 1886. Courtesy of the National College of Arts Archives, Lahore.

DETAILS OF SCREEN, SOUTH SIDE OF BOMBAY COURT.
CONTRIBUTED BY H.H. THE THAKUR SAHEB OF BHAVNAGAR.
Constructed under the supervision of Mr. Proctor Sims, the State Engineer.

DETAILS OF SCREEN, WEST SIDE OF BOMBAY COURT.
CONTRIBUTED BY H.H. THE GAIKWAR OF BARODA.

Raja Ravi Varma (1848–1906)

Going back to the 1893 exhibition, the prize-winning series of ten paintings by Raja Ravi Varma merits discussion. This series represents women from different parts and ethnic groups of India. As mentioned earlier, his one-off paintings were replaced by full-grown, thematic series for exhibition loans.[40] Archival correspondence reveals meticulous discussions between the Maharaja and the artist to arrive at India's own genre of high art.[41] Varma's dedicated study-tours, which were linked with the aforementioned discussions, translated into several sketchbooks that record diverse Indian facial types, costumes and props.[42] Models from these sketchbooks, in addition to live sittings, crystallized in the series sent by Sayajirao to Chicago.[43] Technically, Varma formulated his own way of using oil paints: he mastered the art of chiaroscuro from the European schools and utilized the heavy, impasto technique of the Tanjore School to highlight the jewels and fabrics. Varma also referenced the European originals and prints at the Lakshmi Vilas Palace.[44] He brought a nuanced understanding of the southern Indian dance-dramas, especially Kathakali, to lend animation and stylization to his subjects.[45] This cross-referencing of images and techniques created India's foremost cosmopolitan experiment in high art. Thus while the perceived universal practice of oil painting was heavily indigenized, vernacular traditions such as Tanjore painting and visuals from Kathakali, were placed in a cosmopolitan experiment. The pan-Indian sensibility of these works quite literally evoked a national imagination, which furthers the argument that nationalism need not necessarily be vernacular or antithetical to cosmopolitanism.[46] This explanation from Varma's art extends to the making of the Baroda paradigm, which also anchored the national by courting both the vernacular and the cosmopolitan.

Conclusion

It might be said that this provincial crucible called Baroda was able to host a national ambition and produce some of the finest works for international display and gift exchange. Sayajirao's cosmopolitan model was neither entirely universalizing nor absolutely particular. The Baroda paradigm maintained local differences between craft products coming from various districts within the state, while simultaneously conceiving a pan-Indian high art or generic Indian design.[47] All the same, through its accommodation of mechanization in craft and realism in painting (Western scientific standards of art-craft production), this new category carved its niche beyond Baroda and colonial India. And if cosmopolitanism is about imagining one's place in the larger world,[48] then Baroda made a position for itself at multiple intersections: those of region, nation and colonial empire. The state was affiliated to its many smaller districts, to India and to the larger mechanized Western world and international markets. While through its machine-produced crafts Baroda used industrial standards of Euro-America to measure the quality of goods, it also pitched Indian design as an alternative global standard. Through Ravi Varma's characters, who were dressed in pan-Indian costumes and placed in pan-Indian settings, Baroda became the carrier of a national imagination; in retaining the design portfolios of local artisans, Baroda maintained its vernacular identity. Additionally, through its integration of plural local communities such as "high" artists, caste-based artisans and workshop masters, Sayajirao's model could become a carrier of the national.

Social theory has viewed aesthetic cosmopolitanism as associated with art and hence beyond the realm of experience, ethics and social reality.[49] However, this study on Sayajirao and Baroda demonstrates how the aesthetic can facilitate projects with ethical responsibility and political meaning. Thus when seen at individual levels, Baroda's art commissions drew on diverse tropes and embraced new materials, techniques and themes. And when seen together as a cluster of representative arts and crafts, there was a tenacious inclusion of high-art experiments with craft, design and workshop-style production. The inclusive character of Sayajirao's experiments and their global circulation make one question: Was Baroda's cosmopolitanism truly provincial?

Among colonial India's approximately 15 directly British-ruled territories and 629 princely states,[50] Baroda was but one province. While it was one of the five wealthiest princely states of the time, it was not a port, a centre for trade or a presidency town. In that sense it was not a thriving urban or political centre like Calcutta, London or Bombay, and was hence provincial. However, when appraised for its many modern and alternative experiments in governance, social welfare, health-care and education, Baroda was exemplary. Moreover, in the connections it forged with the rest of India as well as the metropole and other cities overseas by lending its art works and sharing its design aesthetic, Baroda was hardly provincial. This gives value to the point, "Cosmopolitanism is about engaging with others and is to be found in locations that are not necessarily global spaces."[51] Hence while Baroda was not necessarily global it was able to make global connections and utilize international channels for production and dissemination of its art works.

Baroda thus re-ordered itself from one among 629 indirectly ruled British Indian provinces to an internationally recognizable "provenance", a centre for art and craft production and patronage. Its representative art and craft genres were neither mimetic

11
Raja Ravi Varma's 1893 *Portrait of a Lady* is akin to his renditions of the royal Gaekwad ladies in its details such as the Paithani sari, nosering and upper earring, suggesting a distinctly Maratha provenance. Oil on canvas, 120 x 86.3 cm. Collection: National Gallery of Modern Art, New Delhi, Accession No. 1670. Courtesy of the National Gallery of Modern Art.

nor derivative, and so succeeded in expressing a certain independent political position within a colonial space. And Sayajirao's wide embrace of local and non-Indian art forms ensured that the Baroda paradigm of art did not remain conservative or restricted but became truly cosmopolitan.

Notes

1 George Birdwood, *The Industrial Arts of India*, London: Chapman and Hall Limited, 1880, pp. 179, 206, 264, 284, 310.

2 George Watt, *Indian Art at Delhi, 1903: Being the Official Catalogue of the Delhi Exhibition 1902–1903*, London: John Murray, 1904, pp. 14, 34, 58, 61, 62, 84, 85, 152, 156, 184, 195, 204, 218, 251, 257, 258, 330, 332, 337, 444, 482, 484.

3 Gujarat State Archives/Southern Circle, Vadodara/Huzur Political Office (GSA/SCV/HPO): Section 65, Daftar 112, File 8-A: *Exhibitions*: Circular No. 15/5-8 Ex. Extract of the 1886 Colonial and Indian Exhibition Report.

4 Ibid., Letter 610, From: Dewan Kazi Shahabudin, Huzur Cutchery, August 31, 1885, To: Captain J.H. Sadler.

5 Ibid., Letter 34, From: Captain J. Hayes Sadler, President of the Exhibition Committee, April 2, 1886, To: Major T.H. Jackson, Officiating Agent Governor General Baroda; Letter 4938, From: Kazi Shahabudin, April 4, 1885, To: Captain J.H. Sadler.

6 Ibid., Inventory; GSA/SCV/HPO: Section 65, Daftar 111, File 7: *Exhibitions: Exhibitions General Correspondence (1900–1915)*: Precis Report of Three Exhibitions (1886, 1893 & 1900) attached to Letter 5324, From: Chief Engineer of Baroda State, Name illegible, Huzur P.W. Department, Baroda, February 10, 1903, To: St. Louis World's Fair, 1904.

7 I reiterate that these categories are not mentioned per se in the inventory; they are formulated by me to emphasize the various segments within which the loan items may be located.

8 GSA/SCV/HPO: Section 65, Daftar 111, File 5: *Exhibitions: Chicago Exhibition (1892–1895)*: Chicago Exposition Business, From: S.J. Tellery & Co., Delhi, July 27, 1892, To: The Agent, Governor General, Baroda; Letter from: S.J. Tellery & Co., Delhi, August 11, 1892, To: Dewan, Baroda State, Baroda.

9 Ibid., Letter From: Huzur Kutchery, Baroda, October 8, 1892, To: S.J. Tellery & Co.; Letter From: S.J. Tellery & Co., September 30, 1892, To: The Dewan of Baroda State.

10 Ibid., Inventory; List of articles to be presented to the Museum at Chicago in conformity with Huzoor order dated April 23, 1892 out of the Exhibits sent to the Chicago Exhibition 1893; GSA/SCV/HPO: Section 65, Daftar 111, File 7: Precis Report.

11 Gerard Delanty, "Introduction: the Emerging Field of Cosmopolitanism Studies", in Delanty, ed., *The Routledge Handbook of Cosmopolitanism Studies*, London and New York: Routledge, Taylor and Francis Group, 2012, pp. 1–8 (see p. 2).

12 Ibid.

13 Ibid.

14 Owen Jones, *The Grammar of Ornament*, New York, Cincinnati, Toronto, London, Melbourne: Van Nostrand Reinhold Company, 1856; Arindam Dutta, *The Beauty of Bureaucracy: Design in the Age of its Global Reproducibility*, London: Routledge, 2006.

15 Sayajirao had similar ideas which encouraged new development in areas of education, health-care, governance, wealth-accumulation and infrastructure. Together, these ideas made for a holistic plan which imagined an independent and self-reliant princely state as well as nation. See

Priya M. Jaradi, "Fashioning India's National Art: Baroda's Royal Collection, Art Institutions and Crafts at Colonial Exhibitions (1875–1924)", unpublished thesis, National University of Singapore, 2012, Chapter 1.

16 Nikos Papastergiadis, "Aesthetic Cosmopolitanism", in Delanty, 2012, pp. 221–22.

17 GSA/SCV/HPO: Section 65, Daftar 111, File 6: *Exhibitions: Poona Fine Arts Exhibition (1879–1896)*: Letter 45, From: Raja Sir T. Madava Row, Dewan's Cutchery, Baroda, August 5, 1878, To: The Honorary Secretary, Fine Arts Exhibition, Poona.

18 Ibid., Memo with letter 45; Letter 133, From: T. Madava Row, Dewan's Cutchery, Baroda, August 9, 1878, To: The Honorary Secretary, Fine Arts Exhibition, Poona; GSA/SCV/HPO: Section 65, Daftar 111, File 4: *Exhibitions: Simla Fine Arts Exhibition (1879–1895)*: Memo with letter 6140, From: T. Madhava Row, Baroda, July 15, 1879, To: Major Anderson.

19 Ibid., Memo with letter 651, From: T. Madhava Row, Baroda, September 2, 1879, To: Major Anderson.

20 GSA/SCV/HPO: Section 233, Daftar 345, File 2: *Industries: Correspondence Regarding the Manufacture of Pottery*: Memo 587 signed by Dewan T. Madava Row, Dewan's Office, Baroda, February 1877.

21 F.A.H. Elliot, *Gazetteer of the Bombay Presidency, Volume VII, Baroda, Under Government Orders, Bombay*, Bombay: Printed at the Government Central Press, 1883, prefatory page.

22 Speech by Sayajirao Gaekwar, "The Revival of Industry in India: Delivered at the Opening of an Industrial Exhibition at Ahmedabad on the 15th of December 1902", in Anthony X. Soares, ed., *Speeches and Addresses of Sayajirao III, Maharaja Gaekwar of Baroda*, London, Bombay, Calcutta, Madras: Oxford University Press, Humphrey Milford, 1933, pp. 37–75 (see pp. 38, 63).

23 This link between the normative or abstract ideas of cosmopolitical thought and their empirical realization is a concern for contemporary writers, as Western cosmopolitical thought is seen as wanting in empirical grounding. See David Inglis, "Alternative Histories of Cosmopolitanism: Reconfiguring Classical Legacies", in Delanty, 2012, pp. 11–24 (see pp. 12–13, 21–22).

24 Makarand Mehta, "Science versus Technology: The Early Years of the Kala Bhavan, Baroda, 1890–1896", *Indian Journal of History of Science*, Vol. 27, No. 2, 1992, pp. 145–70. Kalabhavan is now part of the M.S. University campus; the original building constructed before 1890 is Senapati Bhavan today.

25 Ibid., pp. 157, 161.

26 Ibid., p. 162.

27 GSA/SCV/HPO: Section 65, Daftar 111, File 5: "A short history of the origin, general organization and progress of Nazarpaga Workshops" by A.M. Masani, Vidyadhikari, September 17, 1909.

28 Ibid.

29 GSA/SCV/HPO: Section 65, Daftar 111, File 7: Letter 100, From: Manibhai J., Glenview, Ootacamund, August 22, 1902, To: Rao Bahadur R.V. Dhamnaskar, Minister, Baroda.

30 Delanty, 2012, p. 2.

31 Dutta, 2006, pp. 2–7.

32 Amin Jaffer, *Made for Maharajas: A Design Diary of Princely India*, New Delhi: Roli Books, 2007.

33 P. Orr & Sons, Swami Catalogue, cited in Vidya Dehejia, "Whose Taste? Colonial Design, International Exhibitions, and Indian Silver", in Vidya Dehejia, ed., *Delight in Design: Indian Silver for the Raj*, Ahmedabad: Mapin Publishing, 2008, pp. 8–19 (see p. 13).

34 Ibid.

35 GSA/SCV/HPO: Section 99, Daftar 127, File 10: *Correspondence with Merchants, Etc: Messrs. P. Orr & Sons, Madras*: True Extract from a note by Major Mant, October 7, 1880 in Letter 2195,

From: Rajah Sir. T. Madhava Rao, Dewan's Cutchery, Baroda, November 25, 1880, To: Messrs P. Orr & Sons, Madras.

36 Sheldon Pollock, "Cosmopolitan and Vernacular in History", in Gerard Delanty and David Inglis, eds., *Cosmopolitanism: Critical Concepts in the Social Sciences*, Volume III, London and New York: Routledge, Taylor and Francis Group, 2011, pp. 365–96 (see p. 385).

37 GSA/SCV/HPO: Section 65, Daftar 112, File 8-A: *Exhibitions in London (1884-1911)*: Letter 34, From: Captain J. Hayes Sadler, President of the Exhibition Committee, April 2, 1886, To: Major T.H. Jackson, Officiating Agent Governor General Baroda; B.A. Gupte, "The Baroda Court", *Journal of Indian Art and Industry*, London: W. Griggs, 1886, pp. 82, 126–33 (see pp. 82, 128).

38 Gupte, 1886, pp. 126–33 and unnumbered colour plates that follow the article.

39 Carol Breckenridge, "The Aesthetics and Politics of Colonial Collecting", *Comparative Studies in Society and History*, Vol. 31, No. 2, 1989, pp. 195–216 (see pp. 211–12).

40 Jaradi, 2012, p. 116.

41 Ibid., pp. 119–20.

42 Ibid., p. 115.

43 Ibid., p. 120.

44 Ibid., p. 124.

45 Priya Maholay-Jaradi, "Raja Ravi Varma: A Study of the Influence of Classical Indian Dance and Literature on His Works", in Ratan Parimoo and Sandip Sarkar, eds., *The Historical Development of Contemporary Indian Art*, New Delhi: Lalit Kala Akademi, 2009, pp. 43–49.

46 Kant, Hegel and Fichte's writings regard the nation as facilitating the final cosmopolitan condition. Cosmopolitanism too facilitates nation-building as seen in 19th-century Europe; only towards the end of this century do nationalism and cosmopolitanism become counter to each other. Bo Strath, "World History and Cosmopolitanism", in Delanty, 2012, pp. 72–84 (see p. 73).

47 The coexistence of national vernacularity which preserves local differences as well as a multinational cosmopolitanism is known. Pollock, 2011, pp. 366–67, 369.

48 Papastergiadis, 2012, p. 226.

49 Monica Sassatelli, "Festivals, Museums, Exhibitions: Aesthetic Cosmopolitanism in the Cultural Public Sphere", in Delanty, 2012, pp. 233–44 (see p. 237).

50 Ian Copland, *The British Raj and the Indian Princes: Paramountcy in Western India, 1857–1930*, New Delhi: Orient Longman, 1982, p. 1.

51 Delanty, 2012, p. 6.

Cosmopolitanism Articulated: The Evolution of Architecture from Wada to Palace

Christopher W. London

Baroda, like all Indian cities, expanded greatly and changed significantly in the 19th- and early-20th-century British period. Its extensive transformation was realized through both admirable administrative structures and significant economic investments. Its fascination with new architectural forms can clearly be traced first to the development of the wada house style. The thirst for architectural novelty led to urban growth anchored in the broad exchange of ideas, and access to new materials, styles, architectural elements and designers, unheard of in earlier eras. The 19th century saw extraordinary architectural output alongside reforms in town planning, transportation, law, education, health and other fields. Extensive building projects for both the rulers and those governed resulted. In particular, the farseeing and progressive-minded Sayajirao Gaekwad III (r. 1875–1939) invested in the future of his state, city and subjects, while he also modified and added to his own domestic quarters. The changes supported architects, required much building activity and irrevocably established the progressive city firmly rooted there today.

The Wada

The architectural features of "modern" Baroda are based upon and evolve from an underpinning of much notable development from the mid- to late 18th century. In this epoch the Maratha wada house type, now rare in Baroda, grew in popularity and developed in splendour, primarily for the domestic needs of an aristocratic and wealthy circle, and also for religious uses. The wada, like its Gujarati/Rajasthani parallel, the haveli, is a large house traditionally built of wood, and possessed of a chowk (interior courtyard space), several floors and elaborate decorative woodwork finishes. Characteristically, the house employs a visibly expressed wooden frame, often carved to a level of great beauty, sometimes with a narrative association. Upper storeys are customarily cantilevered out over the floor below, when desired, to establish balconies for walkways or outdoor space, where needed. The overhang also prevents or diminishes the entry of sun, attendant heat and rain into the building.

In 1824–25 Bishop Heber travelled to Baroda, and observed that the ruling family resided in a wada: "The palace, which is a large shabby building, close to the street, four stories high, with wooden galleries projecting over each other, is quite a specimen of its kind."[1] The architecture described by Heber, as a building type, and in its use of woodwork, "was indeed unusual … and the vernacular architecture of this region was quite distinct from that of the north".[2]

Wadas seem to receive their particular name from their Maratha roots and patrons. Their association with palaces in western India adds interest to the origin of the name. The word wada seems to be derived from "wad", which means a ruling clan in Maratha culture. So, Marathawad or Gaekwad would refer to a royal Maratha clan, as in the title used for the ruling family at Baroda. The palace of such a ruler or prince was often called a rajwada, of which there is a splendid example in Indore dating from 1766, though partly rebuilt. It rises to six storeys above the ground floor, and such exaggerated height surely indicated social status. Its designers were highly specialized Muslim builders who had fled to Indore from Mandu.[3] The Indore Rajwada exhibits some characteristic features of the wada type: it has a large centralized wooden door on the principal elevation, interior courtyards with otlos or raised areas for sitting and business, jharokas (overhanging enclosed balconies) and chhatris (pillared pavilions surmounted by domes). These are combined with more specialized palace features like carved stone and wooden jalis (perforated screens).

Wadas were used and developed in two ways: some were multi-family dwellings, rather like an apartment building, and some were single-family homes occupied by richer and perhaps more commercial or patrician households. Each of the two extant wadas of Baroda studied here seems to have been a single-family building. Like havelis, they were just grander versions of the urban house:

> The final development of the urban house resulted in the *haveli* – a word of Persian origin which denotes a great mansion associated with wealth, status and size. In architectural terms the *haveli* was merely a very grand version of the common house … the increase in size was achieved by duplicating parts … the difference between the *haveli* and the common urban house was one of degree, not of kind, i.e. the difference was quantitative not qualitative.[4]

The area north of the Narmada river in north Gujarat was never well supplied with forest or good timber. As a result, Baroda's wada building materials came from timber imported by sea, with origins in Daman, Malabar or even Burma. Prior to 1853 and the rise of British control, V.S. Pramar states that the Panch Mahals area and the Dangs of south Gujarat had some good teak, but it was soon exhausted and unavailable.[5] Consequently, even in the 17th century, wadas were costly houses, as wisely noted by Jean de Thevenot, a French traveller to Surat in 1666–67.[6] And, by the 1700s and following, constructing a wada became even more costly as the architectural form evolved to become more sophisticated. The costly building materials and the wada's client-underwriters of consequence seemed to combine to demand greater size and more complex spaces with more elaboration to the carving and in some cases rich decorative programmes of paintings framed to cover entire interior walls. In response, specialized teams of designers, builders and craftsmen travelled to Baroda for this work, much like medieval European cathedral builders moving from city to city for the employment of their skills. The establishment of this custom in more important building projects made the use of an architect seem natural to the 1860s' Baroda elite.

Teak became the essential wood employed in wada construction. It was not merely a luxury; its remarkable strength and durability were needed structurally to build upwards,

1

Makarpura Palace, the shade house and formal terraced lawns and flowerbeds. From *Views of Palaces and Places of Interest in Baroda*, by V.G. Chiplonkar, active 1900s. Gelatin silver print, c. 1903. The Alkazi Collection of Photography.

2
Rajwada, Indore, built in 1766, main entrance elevation. Photograph: Vraj Mistry.

as there were no local materials to substitute for this. Later, cast-iron and then steel frames came to fill the architectural and structural need for reinforcement and, in Gujarat, protection from earthquakes.[7] Indeed, Pramar states that in 1820, "in the older quarters of Broach, Cambay, Baroda, Kapadvanj and Patan, virtually every house used wooden framing in a major way …. In Surat, each storey of a building is built so as to be independent and self-supporting. The weight of the building rests not on the brick walls, but on the large wooden pillars, placed at the corners and at intervals along the inner walls."[8] He goes on to state that these houses were "ornamented with much rich and finely cut woodwork. From their fondness for this part of the town and the want of open sites, the families, as they grew larger, added storey on storey to the old houses …."[9]

3
Tambekar Wada, entrance elevation. Note the irregular massing patterns, the overhang on each upper floor, with fine woodcarving, carefully carved struts and other thoughtful detailing.

The two extant wadas examined here are Tambekar Wada and Bhaskarrao Vithal Wada. Other elegant wadas of this calibre, like the Kathiawad Diwanji Dighe Wada, have been destroyed by a growing city that lacks a programme of curating and preserving its architectural heritage.[10] The two surviving structures employed thin bricks set with lime mortar for their walls, supported by wooden columns set atop stone bases to avoid water penetration and insect infestation. Houses of this type often also employed rough black basalt floors in combination with brick paving, each of which made for a surface that could be cleaned easily.

Tambekar Wada, built in the mid-19th century, was the residence of Bhau Tambekar who served as Dewan of Baroda state from 1848 to 1854. It possesses some of the typical characteristics described above: a centrally placed doorway on its principal facade, and wooden vertical structural elements that define each bay of the main elevation. Through a subtle asymmetrical rhythm in the spacing of these elements – bays of typical and wider widths alternating to the left of the main door, while the bays to the right are equal, with half-bays at the end corners – a lively result is achieved from what would otherwise be a fairly static formula. This is further enhanced by an unequally high third storey on the left. That top floor employs handsome arched cut-out trims in wood inside rectangular openings, and above the round-topped door of its inset structural walls. Other features

that enliven the facade are unbroken horizontal lines of timber, cut into ogee moulding, running above the doorframes on each but the uppermost level, and exposed horizontal supporting timbers inset under the roof of the second floor. The horizontal line of timber is most delicately carved at the ground floor, while simpler above. The carved structural brackets of the first and second floors' projecting covered corridors, and their elegant turned woodwork, the delicate wooden and later installed cast-iron railings of the principal elevation, and the oval oeil-de-boeuf, or bull's-eye windows, seen in conjunction with turned and decorative finely carved brackets on the upper floors, all combine to make a character-filled facade. This description also gives clues to the history and evolution of the wada in the mid-19th century. For although some part of it may be of an earlier date, its use of newer elements, like cast-iron railings and bull's-eye windows, indicates the wish of its owners to stay "current" with architectural fashions.

4
Tambekar Wada, reception room with extraordinary painted decoration.

The interior of Tambekar Wada is also noteworthy for its fine and elaborate decoration. Here, on an upper floor, an array of wall-paintings is found in a grand reception room of the residential area. This surviving decoration indicates that initially just the woodwork was painted: the doors, and visible structural beams of the walls and ceilings. All of these are covered with handsome "Hindu"-themed polychrome decoration. Adjacent to them, on the middle of the three bands of horizontal decor levels in one room, there are also small inset ledges with arched openings, for oil-lamps or god-stands, and wooden coat-pegs. These earlier wall-paintings, as also the inset wooden multi-panelled doors, depict either stories of Hindu gods or generic themes depicting romantic couples. Later, more wall-paintings were commissioned for the room, and these include painted "picture frames" in their design, and depictions of foreigners identifiable by their clothes and occasionally by the themes of the pictures. These works seem to draw inspiration from European prints

5
Tambekar Wada, wall of reception room with arched openings, coat hooks and recessed panels.

6
Tambekar Wada, wall of reception room, showing the strong interest in European styles and fashions and their fusion here with Indian narrative and decorative traditions.

and their aesthetic, and the subjects of several are most intriguing. The result is a rich and busy interior, full of narrative interest and contrasting colours and patterns.

It has been suggested that painters worked simultaneously on miniature paintings and on murals for Maratha mansions.[11] In Baroda, several guilds of woodworkers and masons contributed to vernacular architecture.[12] All these craftspeople may be loosely seen as representing a Baroda School, a minor offshoot of the Maratha idiom established at Kolhapur and Poona.[13] It is interesting to note that similar guilds of painters and woodworkers were commissioned alongside European glass- and mosaic-workers in the building of the Lakshmi Vilas Palace.

The specific preference for Hindu-themed decor in Tambekar Wada, and the overall finish to the interior, resurfaces in mutated form in later palace buildings. Interestingly, what begins to appear here as merely a curiosity about Europeans and their fashions, grows to exhibit a specifically European focus in the palaces – either in architectural detail or, in the domestic uses the palaces are designed for, so as to entertain and accommodate the foreign presence in India. This is a pan-Indian 18th- and 19th-century phenomenon. Now under the care of the Archaeological Survey of India and used as the office of the Conservation Assistant, the future of Tambekar Wada is assured, even if its care is not perhaps of the highest level.

Bhaskarrao Vithal Wada is a less complete and less elegant stylistic example of this architectural form. It has a larger footprint than Tambekar Wada, with a spacious adjacent

7
Bhaskarrao Vithal Wada, view showing the otlo that runs along the entire side length of the house, up to the courtyard entrance. Also seen is the wada's general massing and cantilevered structural framing.

8
Bhaskarrao Vithal Wada, large double-doors in the painted arched entrance to the house, with a smaller single door in the right panel.

courtyard that was no doubt integral to the house and its functions when built. The enclosed area of this "yard" has another observable characteristic feature of many wadas, an otlo. This is a raised plinth integral to the structure and plan of the house, extended as a platform from the entrance wall into the interior courtyard, for sitting out or to facilitate the unloading of goods.[14] Here, the otlo extends on either side of the original main entrance: a pair of handsome and carefully detailed wooden doors in a matching doorframe, surmounted by a now painted-over Ganesha figure and carefully carved fruiting vines. These large double-doors overlay onto one another seamlessly, and cut into the right one is a smaller single door, for people rather than carts or carriages. The doorway is in turn integrated into an arched opening, with another Ganesha figure inset in the central recess above, this time surrounded by Garuda, Hanuman, and other attendants. In the two accompanying side pilasters, recesses for lamps are provided. The upper floors

9
Bhaskarrao Vithal Wada, view of inner courtyard.

10
Bhaskarrao Vithal Wada, handsome carved supporting brackets for the first-storey corridor of the main interior courtyard.

11
Bhaskarrao Vithal Wada, view looking up from the inner courtyard.

in this two-storey wada seem to have been allowed to decay, and much of the decorative woodwork removed, though the second (uppermost) floor retains some of its period turned and carved forms. The first floor has lost its cantilevered walkway, and railings and sheet metal obscure much of the original roof details and appearance.

Appreciating the design of these two representative traditional buildings, each erected on a grand scale, should help provide an architectural context for the subsequent changes seen in the royal residences of the Baroda court. These very different buildings, constructed with full access to the amenities and material developments of the 19th century, embrace a new series of social function, Western manners and building technologies in their built fabric and floor plans. They document the transition from Indian sensibilities and needs to a more Western curiosity and subsequent set of focused stylistic desires.

The Palace

Until its demolition in 2014, the **Nazarbaug Palace** provided an excellent example of how the European style was developed to a high standard for the royal family. The building was planned and built to appear as if it sat in a large garden-compound. Yet, despite giving that distinct impression, its bulk was really not far from the compound wall. Consequently, though its occupants would have felt quite removed from the atmosphere of the physical townscape, actually they were not. Its windows looked onto a park, its large entrance gates and high boundary railing all working to close out the city. But, having been rebuilt from an older structure, Nazarbaug was still a transitional work, and the European desire to be "removed", ideally in a large compound setting, was limited by the older palace's site and structures. Nevertheless, Nazarbaug represented a major shift from how the wadas functioned and looked architecturally and contextually, stitched into the townscape as they were. But, more changes were to come later.

The first palace at Nazarbaug was built in 1721. This was completely and splendidly rebuilt by Gaekwad Maharaja Malhar Rao (r. 1870–75). The new building was of white stucco and at its tallest was three storeys high. Constructed in an ornate Italianate style, fluted and plain engaged columns with Corinthian capitals and delicate filigree friezes were employed, with panels and swags added for further decoration. There were also large bow-fronted windows and porches, oriel balconies, multiple pairs of oversize applied console brackets atop columned terraced areas, a capacious porte-cochere at the main entrance staircase, handsome etched-glass windows and a double-height round arch arcade used to enliven the facade, among other features. Eschewing symmetry, the massing for the main central section rose to two storeys, with a drop to a single storey for large areas, and it pushed out in all directions to create a lively and animated facade. Accenting this yet further was a fanciful roofline, capped by urn shapes combined with fan forms that were suggestive of peacock tail feathers, yet also vaguely akin to Islamic arched openings. Jhilmils, or projecting canopies, also appeared throughout the facade. So although the palace seemed European in style, it still employed distinctly Indian innovations and adaptations, grounding it as a work of architects practising particularly in the subcontinent.

Its interiors were equally lavish and Italianate in style, with rooms like the Durbar Hall boasting oversize crystal chandeliers. The palace also had a Shish Mahal, or mirror room, which came from the earlier palace on the site. The gardens were similarly European, designed to appear distinctly formal and continental, with bedding plants, circular fountains,

12
Nazarbaug Palace, main garden entrance elevation, with double-height round arched arcades on ground and first two storeys. Photograph: Kalu Bharwad.

13
Nazarbaug Palace, entrance with a collapsed porte-cochere, bow-fronted bay window to drawing room, and the drawing room elevation facing the garden at right. Note as well the remaining urn and fan form of penetrated stonework on the top terrace. Photograph: Kalu Bharwad.

large lawns and axial vistas to connect the palace to its "fashionable" surroundings. In the grounds, near the main entrance, there was a large stucco octagonal gazebo shaped like a bandstand, in the same Italianate style as the main palace, where musical performances were likely heard. The entrance was through a pair of handsome square stuccoed gate lodges, with impressive ornate cast-iron gates, and the stucco boundary wall was capped for large sections by a cast-iron railing. The building was demolished in 2014, as I wrote this piece; in its last years it lay in disrepair; unpainted, with its windows broken or bricked up and its contents removed.

14
Nazarbaug Palace, main carriage entrance elevation with the collapsed octagonal gazebo in the foreground. Photograph: Kalu Bharwad.

The **Makarpura Palace**, like its older sibling, is designed in the Italianate style. But, here the structure is boldly multicoloured, far larger, appearing more Venetian, and far more restrained and symmetrical in composition on its principal front elevation. It employs a distinctly decorative skyline, and it has formal European-style gardens. It also sits well inside a much larger garden compound than Nazarbaug. Since the Makarpura Palace came later than Nazarbaug, it is liberated from earlier ideas about siting. Instead, it capitalizes upon the opportunity to build in an aristocratic "compound"-like setting of extensive grounds. The whole evokes something closer to Prince Albert's architectural principles and multi-towered model, seen at Osborne House on the Isle of Wight. Makarpura, like Osborne, was conceived as a summer palace, though hardly used as such, the family customarily going to the Nilgiri hills of Tamil Nadu in the hot months.

The palace was built in two phases. Begun in 1870, at the end of Maharaja Khanderao's reign (1856–70), it was greatly extended and renovated by Maharaja Sayajirao Gaekwad III. In 1875, aged 12, Sayajirao was chosen by the British Resident to govern Baroda state. Subsequently, his teachers were British and their approach to his upbringing had a distinct focus on the associated liberal tradition of that culture. So, his building and redesigning of Makarpura with the European aesthetic as predominant is logical and not unexpected.

Makarpura employs twin elevations on its two large rectangular side sections. Each of these is two storeys tall, and all the floors are composed of round-arch arcades. Each floor's arcade varies in consistency with that level's pattern and detailing. Each range also has noticeable but subtle corner massing; using setbacks, window variations, railings or other distinctive qualities, with the additional suggestion of a central pediment over a substantial porte-cochere, as principal architectural features. Then, to join these side sections, a setback single-storey centre section was provided, with a four-storey tower erected exactly to mark the mid-point of the whole. The recessed window openings, developed by this arcaded front, prevent the sun and rain from entering the rooms. And, the consistent arcading also helps to develop the somewhat Jacobean appearance of the massing that each side pavilion possesses, when seen on the diagonal, distinct from the larger whole. At the rear of the palace, a rather different architectural impression is provided. Here each wing takes its design predominantly from its functions. The left side is enclosed by a series of overhanging chhajjas, with terraces and a small staircase, which may have been preserved from the earlier palace. On the right, the newer building is completed with complementary massing and in keeping with the front.

The original interior of the palace was very "up-to-date" for its period of construction, employing the late-19th-century British Aesthetic movement style in its decor, furniture and woodwork details. Consequently, abstract floral wallpaper was laid on the underside of the projecting balcony, and with its curved shape the patterns were thus visible to the users of the room underneath it. There were also exquisite inset vertical panels of decoration around window openings, in which a small white circular motif was picked up and reused throughout the wooden dado in the drawing room. Large and small late-19th-century academic paintings, simple hanging light fixtures and a scattering of informal turned woodwork furniture characterized the space.

15
Makarpura Palace evokes Prince Albert's architectural principles and its multi-towered model. From *Views of Palaces and Places of Interest in Baroda*, by V.G. Chiplonkar, active 1900s. Gelatin silver print, c. 1903. The Alkazi Collection of Photography.

A further unusual feature at the palace was the greatly oversize gatehouse made of brick, with cast-iron and cast-stone or terracotta decorative details. The entrance was composed with four resting lions raised on large brick plinths, very substantial gates, a projecting balcony on the first floor with a niche on either side for inset Venus figures, and atop it all a railing and eight urns. The arched entrance was also decorated with cast-stone elements, and it provided an axial vista down a very long straight drive to the palace. The drive was through Makarpura's large park and gardens, comprising ponds and water features, wooded sections, a shade house, elaborate garden pavilions like the Chinese house, and formal terraced lawns and flowerbeds.

Now used as a training school by the Indian Air Force, the Makarpura Palace continues the architectural journey Baroda pursues to both observe and develop upon models found in Europe. This close association relates directly to Sayajirao's education and exposure to Britain and Europe during his adolescence and early adult years, and his expanding tastes. It results in the comforts, technology and customs of his court all adjusting to incorporate this new influence, resource and political power in significant ways. With the construction of Lakshmi Vilas, a zenith in this process is reached.

16
Makarpura Palace, rear view, with each wing's functions dominating the design. The left side is enclosed by a series of overhanging chhajjas, with terraces and a small staircase; on the right, the newer building is completed with complementary massing and in keeping with the front. From *Views of Palaces and Places of Interest in Baroda*, by V.G. Chiplonkar, active 1900s. Gelatin silver print, c. 1903. The Alkazi Collection of Photography.

The **Lakshmi Vilas Palace** is claimed to be the largest private domestic residence erected in the 19th century. Even if it is not, it is exceedingly large, elaborate in plan, luxurious in finish and extraordinary in look: it is a remarkable building. Its name translates to mean "the abode where wealth and prosperity revel". Designed by Major Charles Mant, RE, FRIBA (1839–81) it was begun on January 12, 1880 and completed in 1896 at a cost of over 30 lakh rupees, or 200,000 pounds, approximately 17.5 to 20 million pounds today. It is Sayajirao's great palace, well suited for his very long reign. The building entailed the extraordinary collaboration and intense involvement of two highly gifted architects, Mant and his successor Robert Fellowes Chisholm, FRIBA (1839–1915), and many other assistants and craftsmen.[15]

Mant began his career in India after graduating from Addiscombe and Chatham schools. He joined the Public Works Department in 1857, "about age nineteen", and "travelled out" to India in 1859.[16] He then worked on his first published design, for a High School at Surat, in 1864 [built 1869–71].[17] Designed in an Italianate Gothic style, it is a handsome building, novel for its time and place, but not indicative stylistically of where Mant was ultimately headed professionally. For, while Mant was building this new type of work for India, he also learned Urdu, Gujarati, Marathi and Hindi.[18] By 1868 he had undertaken repairs to the palace of the Rani of Mandvi, and between 1870 and 1872 he completed work on the Rajaram High School in Kolhapur. The Rajaram High School was his first essay in the "Rajpoot" style, and it cost Rs 3.5 lakhs to build. It was this successful initiation that led to his extraordinary development of the style which he brought to an influential and great height with the Lakshmi Vilas Palace, Baroda. Mant designed three more structures in Kolhapur – a clocktower (design published in 1884), the Albert Edward Hospital and the Town Hall.[19] Mant also designed a court house and high school at Bhownuggur (Bhavnagar), an unfinished palace at Cooch Behar in 1875, two small churches at Balasore and Chupra in 1876, a Memorial Monument to the Maharaja of Kolhapur in Florence, John Russell Colvin's Monument in the square facing the Diwan-i-Am of Agra Fort, several medical schools in Bengal, and a college with a hall called Northbrook Hall at Dacca (Dhaka) – originally Mayo College, but now known as Eden College, built in 1873–75 in what came to be called the Indo-Saracenic style.[20]

Many of these projects stemmed from his firm friendship with Sir Richard Temple, a governor of Bombay, whom Mant followed from Bengal to Bombay, when Temple rose in rank and moved there.[21] In 1878 Mant was appointed Conservator of Ancient Buildings in the Bombay Presidency. He also took a teaching position at Bombay's Sir J.J. School of Art, and became its Superintendent in the years 1878–81. While Mant studied and perfected his understanding of Indian architectural styles, he also completed another Italianate Gothic work, his All Saints Church, Malabar Hill (1880–82), the "chapel of ease" for the Bombay governor.[22] He also designed another significant work prior to Lakshmi Vilas, the Mayo Memorial College at Ajmer (1876–79). This school functioned as an Eton College for the princes of India, gaining great exposure to a most receptive, prominent and attentive audience for this new style, and spreading its influence far and wide.[23]

Mant's work at Baroda began with his construction of both a hospital, the Sir Sayajirao General Hospital (aka SSG today), and the State Library, each begun 1876 and completed in 1880, at a combined cost of 30,000 pounds, and a cable-stayed pedestrian bridge in Kamatibaug, which crumbled in 1964 but will hopefully be rebuilt.[24] In 1877, he designed and built the Medical School at Patna, named after Sir Richard Temple, the Normal Training and Vernacular School at Cooch Behar and the Mitford Hospital at Dacca.

Subsequently, in 1878, he began building work on an extraordinarily designed, vigorous Italianate Gothic style hospital (the Chhatrapati Pramila Raje Hospital [CPR], 1876–81) at Kolhapur, and the Joonagarh (Junagarh) High School. Soon, he had commissions for palaces from the maharajas of Kolhapur and Darbhanga (Bihar), and four years later, he was working on a Town Gate in Baroda and on the Lakshmi Vilas Palace.[25]

The precise process by which Mant was awarded such a great contract, and how he specifically came to be entrusted with such a large commission by the Gaekwad and his court advisors, remains a mystery. But surely, the strong relationship of the Maratha Gaekwad's court with the Maratha court of Kolhapur was pivotal, and helped greatly. A royal marriage may also have sparked the direct contact, possibly bringing Sayajirao south to Kolhapur where he would have seen the remarkable new structures that establish Mant's emerging role as the Maratha "architect of choice"' for the 1870s and 1880s.[26] Furthermore, Mant's accomplished development of the nascent Indo-Saracenic style may also have appealed strongly to Sayajirao. But, how the palace grew to be so large in scope and scale for a client only 18 years old, yet who at that age would become the state's ruler, also remains unknown.

The Lakshmi Vilas Palace has a main elevation 530 feet (160 metres) in length, 150 feet (45 metres) in breadth. Its foundation covers roughly 60,000 square feet (5,575 square

17
Lakshmi Vilas Palace, entire main elevation, from the gardens, showing the three porte-cochere entrances, the palace's central tower and its domed Durbar Hall at left. Courtesy of H.H. Maharaja Samarjitsinh Gaekwad.

metres), with 293,000 square feet (27,220 square metres) of living space, and it is set within an extensive walled garden and approximately 700 acre park (283 hectares).[27] Its plan divided the use into three distinct areas, a domed central block for the Maharaja's residential needs, a left-hand portion for the Durbar Hall and state rooms, and a right-hand portion for the zenana, to house his mother and his wife. The Durbar Hall boasted a double-height apartment finished in luxurious materials and tessera tiling by the Venice and Murano Glass and Mosaic Co. (founded 1866 by Antonio Salviati). The domed central feature was built without centring, carried on 12 corbels. The palace was provided with three porte-cochere entrances, one for each area, and colonnades served to adorn it. The building was constructed using cast-iron, concrete, brick, teak for load-bearing structural work, woodwork and windows, and asphalt materials. It was faced in vitreous grey local "Soongah" sandstone, enriched with blue trap stone from Poona, red sandstone from Agra, and yellow trap stone,

18
Lakshmi Vilas, main elevation showing one of the three porte-cochere entrances and the palace's central tower. From *Views of Palaces and Places of Interest in Baroda*, by V.G. Chiplonkar, active 1900s. Gelatin silver print, c. 1903. The Alkazi Collection of Photography.

19
Lakshmi Vilas, the public/Durbar Hall entrance porte-cochere, which indicates the fine ornamental treatment of the entire facade. From *Views of Palaces and Places of Interest in Baroda*, by V.G. Chiplonkar, active 1900s. Gelatin silver print, c. 1903. The Alkazi Collection of Photography.

employed in strings, columns, panels and other adornments.[28] The hoods of windows and the domes employ coloured tiles or white marble with finials and ribs in gold.

The Durbar Hall was constructed with fine plasterwork, marble columns, and alabaster and marble panels, niches etc., and included a wooden screened gallery for ladies to view court proceedings. It also has stained-glass windows by Arthur J. Dix of London, as do the other important rooms of the palace.[29] Though the palace was built chiefly with local labour, Italian craftsmen came to Baroda for 18 months to do the highly specialized tile work. Throughout the palace interior and exterior, exquisitely crafted complex finishes abound. They are seen in: carved wood details for windows on the inside and outside of the palace, inlaid wood ceilings, handsome plain tile and inlaid tile wall panels, vast areas of highly finished tiled floors as in the Durbar Hall, interior courts with tanks and sprayer pools to cool the air and provide a soothing sound, and the fine sculptures by Augusto Felici used in some parts of the residence.

20
Lakshmi Vilas, section of the main elevation, executed in finely carved "Soongah" sandstone with a wealth of detailing. Courtesy of H.H. Maharaja Samarjitsinh Gaekwad.

Despite the main elevation's complexity, there is a carefully constructed symmetry to the individual elements of the three distinct wings, each having a centre and balanced side development around its domed or elevated middle. Mant disrupts this with a tower and more complex smaller elevation details which answer to interior functions, but the concept originates in a very British Victorian approach to dealing with the massing of such a vast building, and is akin to the well-known contemporary sources of Eaton Hall (1870–82) in Cheshire by Alfred Waterhouse, PRIBA (1830–1905), or the more modestly scaled Scarisbrick Hall (1837–45) in Lancashire by A.W.N. Pugin with additions (1862–68) by E.W. Pugin, which had highly elaborate woodwork interiors and the towered massing seen at Lakshmi Vilas.[30] At the time the building was completed, a RIBA (Royal Institute of British Architects) proceeding chaired by a Mr Spiers describing Mant's Kolhapur Palace "stated it as his opinion that Major Mant drew his inspiration from the buildings in the Hindu Saracenic style round Agra, the Jain temples of Ahmedhabad, and the timber edifices in the Goojerat domestic style".[31] Other cultural centres of the Marathas, and places like Bharatpur, Deeg and Mathura, each historically free of great Mughal architectural interference and influence, may also have had some impact on Mant's design and inspired his final decisions on the palace's appearance. With this in mind Philip Davies writes:

> Thus the palace is not Indo-Saracenic at all, but a more precise commingling of locally based styles with details drawn by native draughtsmen …. It is colossal, so large in fact that the building transmutes itself from a Hindu martial architecture, through various Moghul nuances via a flurry of domes taken from Jain sources, towards Gothic and classical references. The materials, craftsmanship and accommodation represent a blending of Eastern and Western cultures appropriate to the dualistic role adopted by the Indian princes at the time, with one foot rooted firmly in the glories of the Indian past and another planted in British and European society.[32]

Mant died in London on September 17, 1881, age 42. He took his own life, perhaps worried about some investments he had made which temporarily foundered, or possibly because of

21
Lakshmi Vilas, interior of the palace showing the fine carved stonework on the arches, inset panels and also the sumptuous marble stone floors. Courtesy of H.H. Maharaja Samarjitsinh Gaekwad.

miscalculation of the foundation costs of Lakshmi Vilas. It may be surmised that he had overworked himself and that a rather obsessive personality conspired with other factors to overwhelm him. Yet, undeniably he left both an extensive and a now underappreciated legacy in India. The costs for all his various completed works totalled in excess of 750,000 pounds.[33]

At Lakshmi Vilas, Robert F. Chisholm carried on the largely incomplete project. Chisholm honoured Mant's vision, making revisions and emendations only where felt necessary. In this way the palace nurtured and furthered another fascinating architectural career, moulded in a significant way by Mant's works, design intentions and groundbreaking experiments with what became the highly regarded Indo-Saracenic architectural style.

The wadas and palaces discussed here transition from an Indian built form elaborated upon, refined and perfected by travelling craftsmen, to European-style edifices with a similar trajectory. Throughout, the examples demonstrate a progression sensitive to outside ideas, fashions and materials, and visual innovation. When new forms are injected into the possibilities of what might be built in Baroda, a deep underlying natural association with Maratha culture remains. While the wadas draw from a wider western Indian architectural pattern, the great 19th-century palace, Lakshmi Vilas, is encyclopaedic in its architectural vocabulary – it breaks new ground and helps to establish the unusual and yet widely popular Indo-Saracenic style of architecture throughout 19th- and early-20th-century British India.

A List of Other Buildings in Baroda Built under Sayajirao

1. The Baroda Museum and Picture Gallery (1892–94), at Sayajibaug, was designed by Robert F. Chisholm.
2. The Baroda College (1880–82), now the Maharaja Sayajirao University or M.S. University, has a campus that was designed by both Sir William Emerson, PRIBA (1843–1924) and Robert F. Chisholm. Chisholm did the main building that cost Rs 830,150. His design here is heavily based upon his earlier design for the Madras Senate House (1874–79).
3. Kalabhavan, now called Senapati Bhavan (built before 1890), has a Palladian neoclassical design, probably based on a more famous earlier published design. It resembles a greatly shrunken version of Wentworth Woodhouse, Yorkshire (architect Henry Flitcroft) or of Woburn Abbey, Bedfordshire (architects Henry Flitcroft and Henry Holland). Sir William Emerson may have designed the building, as he seems to have been working with this sort of massing on the Kothi Offices. But, if Kalabhavan was actually built around 1890, this would be too late for Emerson to have designed it for Baroda.
4. The Anglo Vernacular School (1889), now the Music College, near Sur Sagar Lake and the Railway Station, were both designed by Robert F. Chisholm. Notable details are the amazing elephant frieze inset on the end wall, the skyline achieved through clever massing and the handsome woodwork designs for the wooden structural supports, akin to designs seen on column capitals at the Kothi Offices.
5. The High Court or Shree Chimnabai Nyaya Mandir (1896), now the District Court, was designed by Robert F. Chisholm. It cost Rs 7,43,666 to build and commingles Mughal and Gothic styles.

6. Khanderao Market was built in the Indo-Saracenic style – possibly by the architect Robert F. Chisholm, unknown date.

7. Chimnabai Clocktower and Market was built in 1887, architect Robert F. Chisholm.

8. The City Library of Baroda/Juna Kot (1876): the original building was designed by Major Mant.

9. The Baroda General Hospital/Sir Sayajirao General Hospital (1876): the original building was designed by Major Mant.

10. Pratap Vilas Palace (1914), built to house the New Public Offices, now the National Academy of Indian Railways, was designed by Charles F. Stevens, the son of F.W. Stevens who is best known for Bombay's Victoria Terminus.

11. Kirti Mandir (1936) was built as part of the Diamond Jubilee celebrations of Maharaja Sayajirao Gaekwad III. It is Indo-Saracenic in architectural style, with an E-shape floor plan and a height of 35 metres. It cost Rs 50,000 to construct.

12. Jamnabai Hospital – unknown architect, unknown date.

Acknowledgements

I would like to thank Kamalika Bose, David L. Hutchinson, Danish Kinariwala and Kenneth Topp for their assistance with the preparation of this article.

Notes

1 V. S. Pramar, *Haveli, Wooden Houses and Mansions of Gujarat*, Ahmedabad: Mapin Publishing, 1989, p. 36.

2 Ibid.

3 Information on the Rajwada in Indore, from Wikipedia, 2014. So, these unusual building skills were in a way "imported" to the court by the ruling Holkar family. Or, the ruling family was wise enough and willing to "chance" employing these craftsmen in an endeavour locals could not deliver for them.

4 Pramar, 1989, p. 108.

5 Ibid., pp. 32–33.

6 Ibid., p. 33.

7 Ibid., p. 48.

8 Ibid., p. 34.

9 Ibid., pp. 34–36. For a lexicon of architectural terms for parts of the wada, see pp. 101 and 202.

10 Ibid., p. 114; the Haribhakti family, bankers to the Gaekwads of Baroda also had a wada in Ghadiali Pol, but it is greatly damaged, or now perhaps completely gone.

11 Saryu Doshi, "Miniature Painting", in Saryu Doshi, ed., *Maharashtra: Traditions in Art, Marg*, Vol. 36, No. 4, September 1985, pp. 49–64 (see p. 63).

12 Gulammohammed Sheikh, "The Backdrop", in Gulammohammed Sheikh, ed., *Contemporary Art in Baroda*, New Delhi: Tulika, pp. 17–51 (see pp. 22–24).

13 Doshi, 1985, p. 49.

14 Muktirajsinhji Chauhan and Kamalika Bose, *A History of Interior Design in India*, Vol. 1, Ahmedabad: SID Research Cell School of Interior Design, 2007, see p. 28 for a mapped floor plan of a wada in Ahmedabad. This shows the divisions between public and private spaces on the ground floor plan and a cross-section of an elevation, for the two upper floors, the top one being private quarters.

15 *The Builder*, Vol. 41, December 24, 1881, p. 805 states in a letter of John Fotheringham's that since 1875 he [JF] worked as a Principal Assistant in Mant's office with one other gentleman, an Indian of the "carpenter caste" but unnamed. They produced the details for Lakshmi Vilas and the Kolhapur palace. Originally this unnamed man and his brother trained with and worked for Mant, perhaps since 1868, but in 1875 the brother died and Mant then employed Fotheringham to do his work, starting with him in Calcutta, but moving him with the office to Bombay in 1878. (Chisholm calls him Mr Fotheringay.) Mant lived at Marine Lines during this period in Bombay. Chisholm picked up Mant's work on the palace when the walls had risen to only eight feet. He supervised the rest of the construction and added the design details needed.

16 *The Builder*, Vol. 41, December 10, 1881, p. 718.

22

Lakshmi Vilas, one of the elegant interior courtyards and corridor spaces of the palace, fully ventilated and cooled by fountains and sprayers. Courtesy of H.H. Maharaja Samarjitsinh Gaekwad.

17 See *The Bombay Builder*, Vol. 4, April 6, 1868, and Vol. 4, November 1868, p. 142, illustration, and *The Times of India, Calendar and Directory*, 1864. (On October 22, 1864, Mant's wife had a son.) See also *The Building News*, Vol. 41, December 9, 1881, p. 750, in which the cost of the High School is given as £25,000.

18 *The Times of India, Calendar and Directory*, 1879.

19 For Rajaram High School see *The Times of India*, October 23, 1874; for the clocktower at Kolhapur, see *The Building News*, 1884, p. 669.

20 *The Architect*, Vol. 26, December 10, 1881, p. 380 for a list of Mant's works.

21 *The Builder*, Vol. 41, December 10, 1881, p. 718. In this account of a meeting, Temple speaks at length about Mant and his unique legacy, after a paper by R. Phené Spiers is read. Temple states that he believes Mant is "a born genius" whose buildings' "distinguishing merits were that whereas some of his architectural predecessors transplanted bodily to India European styles, … he endeavoured to hit upon some style which should unite the usefulness as to practical requirements which characterised European buildings, with the taste of the native style, and the style which was the outcome of those efforts he called Hindoo-Saracenic." Temple was Lieutenant Governor of Bengal Presidency in 1874, and Governor of Bombay Presidency in 1877. In 1880 he returned to England, and so could attend and speak in the meeting as quoted here.

22 All Saints was begun on November 25, 1880 and completed January 16, 1882; see *The Times of India,* January 17, 1882. Thus the church was begun while Temple was there, probably at his request and urging.

23 See *The Building News*, Vol. 36, pp. 198 and 474, illustration. See also *The Building News*, Vol. 41, December 9, 1881, p. 750, in which Colonel Sir Andrew Clarke describes how bureaucrats, who cut budgets and/or shrunk his designs to meet cost targets, made Mayo College a serious casualty to these policies, and thwarted the construction of Mant's more bold and extraordinary design.

24 *The Builder*, Vol. 41, December 10, 1881, p. 718, and date correction to 1880 in same of December 24, 1881, p. 805. The two are the hospital and the library. Sachin Sharma, "After 53 years, Kamatibaug's Jhulta Pul to swing again", *Times of India*, November 19, 2013, accessed December 23, 2014.

25 *The Building News*, Vol. 41, September 30, 1881, p. 440, states that the Kolhapur Palace cost £65,000 and covered 100,000 square feet in area, and the Darbhanga Palace cost not less than £160,000. See also *The Building News*, Vol. 41, December 10, 1881, p. 718. *The Architect*, Vol. 26, December 10, 1881, p. 380 cites the Deoghur Block and the Moodsh Palace from this time (1880) built in the "Gujerat domestic style for a hill chieftain".

26 At his death he is called "the Consulting Architect to the Native States of Baroda, Kolhapur, and Durbhungah" – see *The Building News*, Vol. 41, September 30, 1881, p. 440.

27 The gardens were designed by William Goldring (1854–1919), a landscape architect/naturalist/gardener associated with the Royal Botanic Gardens at Kew, London. He was in charge of the Herbaceous Department and served as assistant editor of *The Garden* (1879), among other accomplishments. See: http://www.historyofvadodara.in/p/photo-gallery.html, pls. 89–92, 258.

28 Philip Davies, *The Penguin Guide to the Monuments of India, Vol. II*, London: Viking, 1989, p. 398 states, "The skyline is a riot of ornamental forms and detail. The entrance to the park is through a handsome gateway, which whets the appetite for the architectural feast to follow. The palace is faced in red sandstone from Agra, with dressings of blue trapstone from Pune and marble from Rajasthan. The interior is equally spectacular."

23

Lakshmi Vilas, Durbar Hall showing very fine stained-glass and Salviati tiling on the inset rectangular window surrounds, both elements being used extensively in the palace's decoration. Also note the fine decorative stencilled and gilded ceiling and the handsome carved balcony details. Courtesy of H.H. Maharaja Samarjitsinh Gaekwad.

29 See *The Building News*, Vol. 41, October 28, 1881, p. 560 and illustration. This article has a plan and a detailed description of the palace, relied upon heavily here. For reference to stained-glass artist Arthur J. Dix (1861–1917), see Davies, 1989, pp. 398ff. Other workmen were a Mr Tree from London (plasterer and gilder for the ceilings and walls), and Signor Felici from Italy for the sculptures that decorate the staircase, Durbar Hall and other public rooms. Twelve workmen from the Venice and Murano Glass and Mosaic Co. (which despite its Italian name, also had two British owners, archaeologist A.H. Layard and antiquarian Sir W. Drake) came to Baroda for 18 months to lay the Venetian mosaic floor in the Durbar Hall. By 1878, with their production of a "revived technique" for Roman murrine glass, they had become famous and were tastemakers of their day. For a long detailed entry on the Palace and its building history provided by R.F. Chisholm see: *Journal of the Royal Institute of British Architects*, 1896, pp. 421–33. It lists the following Indian draughtsmen associated with the drawn details of the Palace – Mr Hasjee succeeded by Mr Gumput Singh; and the Clerk of Works – Mr Modi succeeded by Mr Harrischund Gopall. It also lists Chisholm's three design changes to the palace: a flat roof over the Durbar Hall, revisions to the tower and removal of a clock, and changes to the construction materials of the dome.

30 Mark Girouard, *The Victorian Country House*, Oxford: Clarendon Press, 1971, pls. 3, 73 and 75–77.

31 *The Architect*, Vol. 26, December 10, 1881, p. 380.

32 Philip Davies, *Splendours of the Raj, British Architecture in India 1660–1947*, London: John Murray, 1985, pp. 201–03.

33 See *The Building News*, Vol. 41, December 9, 1881, p. 750.

Adventures in Art Education: N.S. Bendre at the FFA

Ratan Parimoo

The spirit of Independence was in the air when the Faculty of Fine Arts was started at Baroda in 1949/1950 by the newly established Maharaja Sayajirao University. The FFA began with a clean slate and was completely free from any kind of conservative art school atmosphere, unlike the tedious rendering from plaster casts of antique Greco-Roman sculpture or laborious studies of nude models practised at the Sir J.J. School of Art, Bombay; or the mechanical copying of stylized forms from Ajanta murals or subjecting watercolour paintings to repeated "baths" in the Bengal wash technique associated with Santiniketan. Despite the long hours of discussions that must have gone into the staff or Board of Studies meetings among artist-teachers and external experts at Baroda, there has been no recorded blueprint of objectives or methods of art teaching. Therefore, there is no definite document of art education ascribable to Baroda and this must be deduced from the daily studio and classroom teachings. Perhaps this absence of a blueprint is what led to the assembling of and access to several techniques and media in one campus. Right from the first year, even while doing head-studies or still-lifes, a student was simultaneously exposed to and encouraged to practise more creative compositions.

Two Bombay personalities, N.S. Bendre (1910–92) and V.R. Amberkar (1907–88), were closely associated with Baroda from the outset.[1] I was one of the earliest students of Bendre at Baroda (from 1951) and remember, among others, the lessons he gave over several weeks during my second year, in stylizing the human contour in quick sweeps, akin to Jamini Roy's figural works.[2]

Individual creativity and thinking, as projected by the many revolutionary artists of 19th- and 20th-century Europe, were almost unwritten slogans at the FFA – an attitude inculcated to some extent by the inclusion of a rudimentary art history of various world cultures in the teaching programme. For the first time there was an art institution that did not just focus on art lessons but instead introduced its students to "contemporary art in the making". It is significant that when a Master's degree was introduced in 1954, "Creative Painting" was offered among the four choices in the Painting Department; I opted for this module in 1955. The studios and buildings which gradually came up on the campus during that decade were actually treated as artists' studios, kept open even after office hours, on holidays and during vacations. It was here that one could watch Bendre at work. These post-office studio hours culminated in Bendre's memorable one-man show in Bombay in 1956.

Experiments with Light and Colour

Although Bendre conducted private art classes in Bombay, his experiments in art education matured only in Baroda. And it may also be stated that it was here that he embarked on his serious explorations as a creative artist. Until then he had demonstrated tremendous facility in handling the watercolour medium (especially in the opaque technique called "gouache") and in the use of pastel. He did landscapes and figurative studies in both these media, in what could be called an Impressionist/Expressionist style, as, while revealing a sensitivity for the Indian tropical light and sunshine, his brushwork remained too broad and bold for Impressionism. Obsessed with outdoor landscapes, he painted these in Kashmir and Banaras. Prior to these plein air landscapes by Bendre, there is hardly an Impressionist phase in any Indian painter's work wherein atmospheric effects (generally of sunshine) combine with the breakup of colour in terms of the spectrum. The so-called Indore School of landscape was characterized by opaque watercolour applied in prominent brushstrokes, always subduing the hues and generally preferring wet monsoon effects. With the exaggeration of the hues and even the inclusion of black – which are Expressionist traits – Bendre rather successfully attempted a sort of telescoping of the late-19th-century French Impressionist style with the German Expressionist style of the second decade of the 20th century.

Simultaneously, Bendre also painted extensive series of one-figure studies in the gouache technique, depicting different ethnic Indian types in picturesque costumes, which lend themselves to variegated colour juxtapositions: the old bearded man from Udaipur, or the vivacious village girl, generally shown in informal postures, compare well with the Company School firka paintings (depicting Indian ethnic people engaged in various crafts and occupations) of 19th-century British India, and their later versions.

In some of Bendre's works we observe his efforts to relate naturalism, modernity and traditional style. I think this "will to stylize" perhaps served as a bridge to his bolder experimentation with cubistic language during the 1950s. Also, his travels to the United States during 1947–48 allowed a firsthand acquaintance with 20th-century modern Western art.[3] It appears that things happened very fast with him during these years, paving the way for his subsequent key role in Baroda.

The two elements of colour and line remained predominant in Bendre's work from 1950 onwards. Like several artists of his generation he too emerged as a master of wide-ranging techniques and media, but few developed as broad an outlook as his. His technical versatility, an asset to him as a teacher at Baroda, also makes Bendre unique among the living artists of India. The right combination of such desirable qualities led to his implementation of complete freedom of approach to creative expression at the FFA. This resulted in breaking the inhibitions that had limited artists to work with traditional means, enabling them instead to engage with a variety of materials not hitherto used in the country. In this way, a whole field of new effects and possibilities of configuration opened up and posed young artists with new challenges.

Forays into Cubism

Bendre's cubistic works fall into two distinct groups: human figures and still-lifes. Those based on the human image appear as if the single-figure, multi-hued watercolour firka studies of the 1940s are now repainted in almost monochromatic but receding and

1
Demonstration by N.S. Bendre in the Painting Studio, Faculty of Fine Arts, M.S. University, 1956–57. Collection unknown. Photograph (copy of original): Mahesh Padia.

protruding structural planes, in which, by comparison with the former mode, now the space and figures are firmly interlocked. One is reminded of the transition towards cubism in the works of Picasso, Braque, Gris and Mondrian.[4] What interested Bendre most were spatial tensions and not cubistic distortions. Bendre's cubistic works cannot be classified as analytical or synthetic like the original French developments. But they have a characteristic of their own in their attempt to synthesize the simplicity of human form of Indian miniature paintings with the cubistic structure of receding and protruding planes. In that sense, these have a genuine Indianness about them.

Though in keeping with cubistic structure Bendre usually used low-key colours which have their own symphonic value, like variations of greys or browns, in some cubistic works he introduced bright hues (normally avoided in standard cubism) which served two purposes. One, the Indian-type colour scheme, as yet another facet of Indian miniature painting, was brought into the pictorial construction. Two, the tonal modulation of the hues also suggested the sunshine of the Indian landscape, thus establishing a clear link with his own plein air paintings of the 1940s.

A convincing example of this observation is seen in a comparison of two paintings: *Cow and Calf*, 1948, represents the style of that period, whereas *Complementaries*, 1956, depicting a buffalo and a crane, is a cubistic work. Both are in oils and show similar compositional arrangements: the cow rears its head towards her calf as it leaps towards her teats, much in the

2
Banaras Ghat, by N.S. Bendre, 1940. Watercolour, 38.1 x 76.2 cm. Collection unknown. Photograph: Mahesh Padia.

3
Demonstration of landscape painting by
N.S. Bendre at a ghat in Banaras, during
an FFA study tour, 1953–54. Collection
unknown. Photograph: Mahesh Padia.

same manner as the dark buffalo turns its bulky horned head towards the lean white crane. In the cubistic painting, apart from geometricizing the buffalo's form, a receding plane like a foil is established in the space behind it. In the foreground are the distinguishing elements which make it different from the impressionistically modelled earlier paintings.

In paintings that followed, *Wood Cutter* and *Homeward*, both 1957, Bendre simplified the natural form with slight elongation and tubular limbs. He also altered the background elements to fit with a more cubistic treatment of the space, and employed sharp colour contrasts. These paintings clearly reveal the narrow gap between some aspects of the cubistic language and traditional Indian pictorial practices.

In contrast to his romanticized rural subjects, some of which derived from the shepherds or bharvads of Saurashtra, *Companions*, 1957, depicts a middle-class household, possibly his own family; the mother typically combs the daughter's hair and the peculiar Indian cloth cradle is integrated in the setting. Another variation in his cubistic figurative paintings was when he took themes from Indian sculpture, as in *Thorn*, 1955, which echoes the famous sculpture of a female figure removing a thorn from her foot in a Khajuraho temple.[5] In the painting a female nude is depicted with many flexions of her torso and limbs; the tribhanga (contrapposto) posture fits well with the cubistic approach to handling the figural form, but Bendre adds the dimension of volume and its interaction with space. The conical forms in space stand as cubist planes as well as provide the environmental setting of the mountain and the tree – the latter a motif again derived from the shalabhanjika (well-endowed form of a woman holding a tree/branch, symbolizing fertility) imagery of traditional Indian sculpture.[6]

Bendre's still-life groups in cubistic style of the late 1950s are among his most important paintings. This is my considered view, speaking retrospectively after a lapse of five decades.

4
Old Man from Udaipur, by N.S. Bendre,
1956. Oil on paper, 48.7 x 34 cm.
Collection: National Gallery of Modern
Art, New Delhi, Accession No. 2973.
Courtesy of the National Gallery of
Modern Art.

5
Hindu Pandit, by an unknown artist,
Company Period, early 19th century.
Paper; 16.5 x 12.3 cm. Collection: Lalbhai
Dalpatbhai Museum, Ahmedabad,
Accession No. LDII.1492. Photograph:
Mahesh Padia.

They deserve to be recognized among the most significant set of masterpieces left by a 20th-century Indian painter; no other has done such masterly still-life paintings. *Sun Flower* is quite well known, used on the cover of the Lalit Kala monograph on Bendre published in 1957. Painted as early as 1955, it ushers in his cubistic style, already mature and very characteristic in its simplicity, though otherwise having complex elements like the variation in the relative size of the flowers. Perhaps the greatest masterpiece among the still-life series is *Parrot and Chameleon*, c. 1950, for which Bendre actually arranged a dead chameleon along with other objects. Its reproduction in the Marathi journal *Mauj* of 1955 is the only record we have of this painting.[7] The stuffed parrot perched on a wooden stand is positioned diagonally, but the circular form of its head is echoed by the round mouths of the pots. The dead chameleon below repeats the greenish yellow colour of the parrot while its tail is coiled to conform to the other circular objects. A variation of orange contrasts with the green, while purple and magenta have been used for what are to be understood as planes of shadows, not compatible with European cubist practice.

Bendre's very rich corpus of cubist still-lifes can certainly be considered prized national art treasures and a formidable contribution to international cubism. Quite appropriately he exhibited these works at Baroda and Bombay in a major one-man show in 1956, which may be considered historically as heralding a new epoch in modern Indian art. Unfortunately this fact was not highlighted during the only retrospective exhibition of his works, held in Bombay in 1974 to mark the occasion of a Lalit Kala Akademi Fellowship being bestowed on him.[8]

Some further comments on Bendre's use of colour in his cubist paintings may be relevant here. These paintings are all done in oils and reveal his command over the

6
Cow and Calf, by N.S. Bendre, 1948. Oil on board. Collection: Salar Jung Museum, Hyderabad. Courtesy of the Salar Jung Museum.

7
Complementaries, by N.S. Bendre, 1956. Oil on board; 101.4 x 118.2 cm. Collection: National Gallery of Modern Art, New Delhi, Accession No. 1713. Courtesy of the National Gallery of Modern Art.

medium. His paint surfaces are, literally speaking, beautiful with carefully blended tones and methodically applied colour-changes. He left nothing to chance. There are no smudgy or murky patches. During the teaching sessions, dealing with colour exercises, he would warn against the use of muddy colours, and what he called "raw" colours, i.e. the tone or value of the pigment as it came out of the tube. His exploitation of both the structural and symphonic qualities of colour showed his range as a colourist who invented new nuances. Besides the predominantly Indian subject-matter, often the colour-schemes too

8
Thorn, by N.S. Bendre, 1955. Oil on board; 168 x 119.3 cm. Collection: National Gallery of Modern Art, New Delhi, Accession No. 1136. Courtesy of the National Gallery of Modern Art.

9
Companions, by N.S. Bendre, 1957. Oil on hardboard; 120 x 128 cm. Collection: National Gallery of Modern Art, New Delhi, Accession No. 1761. Courtesy of the National Gallery of Modern Art.

were inspired by those used in miniature paintings or observed from the Indian locale. He devised his own way of modelling with colour modulations and tones, particularly in depicting the Indian female complexion, for which he substituted Indian red or even blue, besides yellow-ochre. He would mellow down or modify the colours to get the most satisfying effect. The muting would be done in such a way that the standard hues would look more like the reds, oranges and mauves of the typical Indian variety. Indian tropical light was effectively re-created in Bendre's landscapes, several of which depicted the fisherfolk of Versova, Mumbai. He also modulated colours to produce sunshine effects on dark Indian complexions, as seen in *Mother and Child* and *Festive Mood* (both 1955), in which green is used for shadows on the complexion and yellow for planes in the sunshine, together with "Indian" colours for saris and blouses.[9]

New Forms and Vocabularies

As argued earlier, his cubo-figurative paintings alone could assure Bendre an important place in 20th-century Indian art. But he was not to stop here. His researches in colour took a new turn around 1958. At the same time, he gave up the earlier preoccupation with Indian subject-matter. He began experiments with drip paint, pouring thick liquid colours on the canvas surface, allowing them to spread out and merge at select places. In conjunction with his formidable sense of design, he brought into play his subconscious,

resulting in strange forms and effects which would normally be impossible to render consciously. But these were only transitory digressions to enable the mind to purge itself of thinking in terms of objects or of subject-matter.

Bendre's plunge into abstraction may seem sudden. But his primary preoccupation with structure and the reduction of things to bare essentials had already bordered on abstraction. If one carefully looks at Bendre's abstract studies (executed during the late 1950s and early '60s but almost forgotten now), one will observe the presence of certain Bendre-esque characteristic traits that are found in his paintings of the 1950s and even in those done earlier.[10] He retains the earlier cubist framework as in *Abstract Form*, 1956, and *Entwined Form*, 1962, while inventing endless combinations of colours and shapes worked out in overall patterns. The colours have a certain coolness about them, predominant being cold blues, purples and greens. In case of warm colours like reds their saturation is changed to make them cooler. The colours bear some amount of volume, spatial recession and at times a linear dimension. The effect on the observer is of effortlessness, ease, spontaneity and abandon.

The Baroda phase not only leads us to arrive at some assumptions regarding Bendre's personality, but also tells us how the trends in his own work shaped his teaching.[11] Although

10
Parrot and Chameleon (Popat ani Sardaa), by N.S. Bendre, c. 1950. Oil on canvas. Collection unknown. Photograph: Mahesh Padia.

11
Abstract Form, by N.S. Bendre, 1956. Oil on masonite board, 122 x 81.2 cm. Collection: Tata Institute of Fundamental Research, Mumbai. Photograph: Anil Rane.

he was what I have called a "typical" artist by temperament with his carefree attitude and minimal involvement with worldly matters, his passion for cubism and abstraction is noteworthy. It was the inherently non-personal aspects of these stylistic vocabularies, including the cold calculatedness of cubism that fascinated him. He rightly believed it to be the key movement of the 20th century; even today most Western critics agree that cubism changed the concept of pictorial structure in the 20th century and that all subsequent art movements had to come to terms with it. Bendre realized a twofold intellectual possibility in cubism. One was the reduction of the three-dimensional world and the compression of it to conform to the two-dimensional surface of the canvas, which required emphasis on structure and simplicity, on bare essentials and avoidance of detail. The second intellectual possibility was a result of Bendre's perception of similar qualities in Indian miniature paintings: in particular, the simplicity, the compression of space and volume, and the division of space.

Art Classes at the FFA

Undoubtedly, Bendre's activity as an artist-teacher became a source of much inspiration. By the late 1950s, some of us Baroda students of the early batches began to mature. While instructing us, he maintained a focus on how we could evolve our own way of seeing things and "complete" the painting. Often he would remark, "All right, you have learnt the colour-scheme and the composition, but now how will you 'treat' it, or 'finish' it?" This is where he wanted the student to think. For all these separate visual problems he would set up exercises and group discussions. At times, while scrutinizing a student's work, exasperated or charged, he would pick up a brush and give a few touches to show how the whole painting could be "resolved". His proven versatility made him a figure of hero-worship among students. His demonstrations were the most exciting occasions in the Painting Studio where in an electrified atmosphere students crowded behind him, climbing on stools and tables to watch him work. Some of us, by then post-graduate students, who were given separate cubicles for work, would wait for his arrival during the morning hours in the hope that he might glance even for a moment at the painting in progress on the easel. An approving nod from him was a joyous event; his smallest suggestion, most laconically spoken, was considered a great blessing.

Bendre's teaching strategy also included compositional exercises especially in shape, texture and tone. One method he used was to cut a photograph first into four sections and then each into further sections. Random sets of pieces were distributed to the students. Whatever set of black-and-white shapes one received, one had to rearrange in a composition of tone and texture. Through such exercises one was able to relate to the works of Matisse for colour and to cubists for collage and abstraction. A course in copying from Indian miniature paintings and Ajanta murals enabled us to observe parallels between Indian and Western art. The Quick Sketching classes once or twice a week were also most memorable, when a model was provided and graduate and post-graduate students worked together.

In his notes on the painting *Parrot and Chameleon* published in *Mauj*, Bendre explains how he arrived at the cubistic transformation of the group of objects. He made a naturalistic drawing as well as stylized drawings to reveal how the shapes are modified to relate in compositional terms or how spacing is readjusted to integrate the objects in structural terms. The fourth and the resolved stage was the finished painting itself. This illustrated record demonstrates the creative process towards the formulation of a clear style. In 1955 this would be among the few records of an art teacher's methods simultaneously relevant to his own creative work.

Many of us having completed our courses would now disperse. It was then that Bendre suggested we should form a Baroda Group of Artists with a view to working and exhibiting together. Although this never truly materialized, some of us continued to study in Baroda under him with the help of the National Cultural Scholarships that had just been instituted under the auspices of the Department of Culture, Government of India. And subsequently in the early 1960s some of us were inducted into the FFA teaching staff, enabling an artists' community to grow in Baroda where there had been none before. Several consecutive exhibitions under the banner of the "Baroda Group" were held in Bombay between 1956 and 1961 and were well received. I remember Shamlal of *The Times of India* used such suggestive adjectives as "Kleever" and "Grisly" (implying that some of the painters were influenced by the works of Paul Klee and Juan Gris) in one of his reviews.[12]

During these years Bendre discussed several dilemmas common to Indian artists. For example, what should be the approach of young modern Indian artists? How does one identify the modern elements in traditional Indian painting? How best can an artist use these as the basis for a synthesis of the two dichotomous modes? Baroda indeed established that institutionalized art training could be geared in such a manner as to make it conducive to the growth of creativity, despite still persisting scepticism about this. In Gujarat, which was an "art-wilderness" at the beginning of the 20th century, the late Ravishankar Raval kindled the flame of creativity through the limited example of traditional Indian painting during the 1920s and '30s. A couple of generations later, during the '50s and '60s, scores

12
Entwined Form, by N.S. Bendre, 1962. Oil on board; 102 x 127 cm. Collection: Lalit Kala Akademi, New Delhi. Courtesy of the Lalit Kala Akademi.

13
Work done during a demonstration
of cubism by N.S. Bendre at the FFA,
1955. Oil on oil-paper; 76.2 x 50.8 cm.
Collection: Painting Department of the
Faculty of Fine Arts, M.S. University,
Baroda. Photograph: Mahesh Padia.

of young artists from Gujarat and other parts of India (including myself from Kashmir)
received their first lessons from Bendre. He opened up the wide horizons of creative
possibilities before them.

Notes

1   Around 1947, Smt. Hansa Mehta (the first Vice Chancellor of M.S. University) was the
    Chairperson of the Bombay Presidency Art Reorganization Committee. V.R. Amberkar
    was Secretary of the Committee. N.S. Bendre, who was one of the members, was persuaded
    subsequently to associate with the new institution in Baroda. The Report of this Committee was
    printed in 1948 by the Bombay Government.

2   This essay briefly profiles the work of N.S. Bendre in the form of a first-person account of my
    years as a student of Painting at the FFA. I have discussed the Baroda School at length in my
    Studies in Modern Indian Art (New Delhi: Kanak Publications, 1975), which is also a first-person
    account of my years as a student and then as a teacher.

3   See Ram Chatterjee, *Bendre: the Painter and the Person*, Toronto: The Bendre Foundation for Art
    and Culture and Indus Corporation, 1990, for a detailed biographical account. However, the
    coverage of Bendre's Baroda period is sketchy and based on secondhand information.

4   See Robert Rosenblum, *Cubism and Twentieth Century Art*, New York: Harry N. Abrams, 1961.

5   Plate 18, in Karl Khandalavala and K.K. Hebbar, eds., *Bendre*, New Delhi: Lalit Kala Akademi,
    1957. It has a brief text by an anonymous writer.

6   This painting of 1955 in tones of sepia or burnt umber was followed by another painting in
    similar colours entitled *Load*, now in the collection of Bharat Kala Bhavan, Banaras University.
    It is an even more complex representation of a multi-flexioned female nude.

7   See *Mauj*, Bombay: Mauj Prakashan, Diwali, 1955.

8   The exhibition was held at the Jehangir Art Gallery, Bombay. The catalogue, edited by Patwant
    Singh, includes a kind of evaluative introduction by V.R. Amberkar, but it is all too brief.

9   See colour plate in *The Illustrated Weekly of India*, July 17, 1960.

10 The first exhibition of Bendre's abstract experiments was held in Bombay in 1959 and a brief
    note was published in *Design Magazine*, Bombay, 1960.

11 *Prof. Bendre, 1986–87, Kalidas Samman*, Bhopal: Bharat Bhavan. This catalogue includes a short
    statement, "My Painting" by Bendre himself.

12 The present author has prepared a docu-account of "The First Baroda Group of Artists", published
    in Gauri Parimoo Krishnan, ed., *Ratan Parimoo: Ceaseless Creativity, Paintings, Prints, Drawings*,
    Singapore and Vadodara: Gauri Parimoo-Krishnan, 1998.

Inverted Hierarchies:
The Work of Jyoti Bhatt

Karin Zitzewitz

Among the most important forces in the history of art after Independence was the need to counter an assumption, put forth periodically by often well-meaning historians and curators, that modern Indian art was a matter of the assimilation of Indian content within Western forms.[1] That supposition is impossible to sustain after any serious consideration of modernism as it was pursued in Baroda.[2] Particularly after the intervention of Group 1890 in 1962–63,[3] artists associated with the Faculty of Fine Arts at the Maharaja Sayajirao University worked consistently to subvert two ideas: one, the impression that forms recognized as modernist were fundamentally foreign to India; two, the premise that form is both distinct from and superior to content. They recognized how these hierarchical judgements, articulated in the language of aesthetics, echoed larger colonial discourses of mimicry. Building on the set of ideas developed in Santiniketan, Baroda artists came to articulate a new and highly productive understanding of artistic form.

Modernism, Baroda Style

After it was founded in 1950, artists teaching at the FFA established a curriculum that was cognizant of and in dialogue with a variety of globally circulating definitions of form. These included both the Bauhaus-derived pedagogies used in the Faculty and looser understandings of the post-war School of Paris, ideas whose presence can be attributed both to the circulation of art-writing and the periodic return of emigre artists from abroad. In the early 1960s, emphasis on the pure materiality of medium articulated in influential movements in Italy, Japan and the United States found echoes in the building up of grit and soil into the pigments used by Baroda oil painters. And so formal change was largely understood as emitting from either the (re)discovery of aesthetic fundamentals *or* tendencies secreted in media in themselves. Against this understanding, Baroda artists began to see form in sociological and historical terms. In a position articulated most forcefully by K.G. Subramanyan (b. 1924), Baroda artists came to expect that modernism could and should be integrated with and continually invigorated by Indian visual culture.

This essay will explore how Subramanyan's call was put into practice, focusing particularly on the work of Jyoti Bhatt (b. 1934). Among Baroda artists, Bhatt was both consistent and deliberate in his commitment to overturning art hierarchies. Originally trained as a painter in oils, Bhatt abandoned the premier medium of the mid-20th century for the less valued practices of printmaking and photography.[4] His strongly modernist sensibilities –

most importantly his affinities for pattern and flatness – informed his printmaking and photography alike. Further, Bhatt saw culture as a set of signifying practices, a position that resonates with the international "linguistic turn" through which structural anthropology was popularized. These aesthetic preoccupations shaped Bhatt's assembling of one of the most important archives of photographs of visual cultural forms in India. But Jyoti Bhatt's prints and photographs are also indicative of a larger approach to modernism in Baroda.

While at first Bhatt used the camera to collect images for use in his other work, he later became motivated by the incipient modernization of the countryside to document folk art practices before they vanished.[5] His surveys were sporadic and informal, undertaken during summer holidays or on weekends off, often in the company of sculptor and photographer Raghav Kaneria (b. 1936). Bhatt is a friendly and affable man, and he became the consummate photographer's guide to Gujarat. He accompanied many of India's finest photojournalists on shoots in the state, taking advantage of their vehicles, travel budgets and technical expertise to continue his own photography.[6] He also photographed the rich regional art traditions of Orissa, Rajasthan, Madhya Pradesh and Bengal, the kolam floor-painting tradition in south India, and the adivasi communities of the Andaman Islands.

The Problem with Virtuosity
Jyoti Bhatt was born in Bhavnagar to a father who was a progressive and nationalist educationalist. After studying in his father's school, Bhatt attended the progressive and nationalist Shri Dakshinamurti Vidyarthi Bhavan. He did not pass his matriculation, refusing on political grounds to take his required exam in English.[7] Nevertheless, Bhatt entered the FFA at the M.S. University in its first batch, studying there until he joined the teaching faculty in 1959. Bhatt was an extraordinarily successful student, demonstrating control over a variety of techniques and styles.

Bhatt's skill was recognized early. He won a national award in 1956 for his painting *Krishnaleela*, 1955. Bhatt's work was entered in the section for "traditional" art, alongside the works of hieratically trained artists, because of its subject matter, narrative conventions, and depiction of figures and foliage. It is modelled on the revivalist Gujarati art and literary movement led by Ravishankar Raval (1892–1977), an artist and editor who flourished in Ahmedabad between the 1920s and '50s. But for all its invocations of tradition, Nilima Sheikh argues, Bhatt's painting evinces a modernist sense of design and ornamentation. Sheikh states that, typical of Faculty-trained artists, Bhatt treats tradition as a compendium of sources which he, "through education and modernist discernment, has learnt to identify and organize".[8] And so, despite its classification in the competition, this painting is marked less by its continuities with traditional forms of painting than by its realization of a break with the past. As Sheikh writes, "notions of good taste intervene."[9]

Bhatt's mastery of the revivalist style of painting promoted by Raval is surprising only because of the contrast it poses to the approach offered at the Faculty by his teacher, N.S. Bendre (1910–92), which Bhatt adopted during his time as a student. Bendre taught his students the fundamentals of composition and design, often demonstrating how they could resolve their paintings by quickly altering the works with his own hand. Bhatt added to Bendre's emphasis on composition and design an interest in surface texture and pattern. His oil paintings in this period focused either on commonplace objects, such as lanterns, or on peasant archetypes. As K.G. Subramanyan notes, even in his early works, Bhatt

1
Self-portrait by Jyoti Bhatt, c. 1980. Photographic print. Collection of Jyoti Bhatt.

2
Krishnaleela, by Jyoti Bhatt, 1955. Watercolour tempera; 45.7 x 182.9 cm. Collection of Jyoti Bhatt. Photograph: Jyoti Bhatt.

had "the kind of talent that readily reconciled calculation with accident".[10] This proved to be an ideal set of skills for printmaking. After a stint studying painting in Italy, Bhatt trained in printmaking at the Pratt Institute in New York City in 1964, supported by a Fulbright scholarship.

In an interview, Bhatt told me that he was attracted to the relative inexpensiveness of making and consuming prints, as well as the way reproducible prints escaped the market associations of paintings. Bhatt's prints are beautiful and meticulous, often relatively modest in scale and seemingly lighthearted in tone. In his most reproduced work, *Lost Pundit,* 1965, an owl sits on the head of a priest whose Vaishnavite affiliations are literally inscribed on his face. The owl, a symbol of idiocy in India and wisdom in the West, is covered in signs of various religions and ideologies: hammer and sickle, Om, cross, yin-yang. In a box on the left, the artist's name is presented in outsized printed letters. The print feels like satire, but it is not totally clear what or who is the target. Is Bhatt commenting on the sectarian practice in which the name of Ram is tattooed on the body? Or, is the owl more important, and does the print find all signs of political and religious ideologies equivalent? Or, does Bhatt's print just value the graphic presence of signs, including the letters that make up his name, in an elevation of surface over depth? All three seem like valid interpretations, especially when *Lost Pundit* is seen alongside other prints in which meaning is evaded altogether through the juxtaposition of signs.

The Act of Documentation
The question of where meaning lies in Bhatt's works is even more complicated in his archive of documentary photography. As mentioned earlier, Bhatt's initial goal as a

photographer was to find sources for his prints and paintings. His professors encouraged him to do so,[11] including Bendre, whom he photographed recording details of Saurashtran dress in his sketchbook much later, in 1981. Bhatt made one of his first trips out with a camera in 1959, to Tarnetar, a fair and pilgrimage site near Surendranagar, Gujarat. One of Bhatt's photographs from 1959, of two young men in traditional Saurashtran shirts and jewellery, is similar in tone to the observational sketching practice of his teacher. But another is strikingly different. Though the image retains interest in ornament and dress, Bhatt had absorbed the lessons of contemporary documentary photography. In contrast with the casually posed snapshot, important for what is in the picture, the other is concerned with how we see the boys. It is an energized composition with a sharp contrast between foreground and background, further animated by the angular juxtaposition of the two figures, and made tense by the hostile gaze of one of the men. This second picture captures a "decisive moment", following Henri Cartier-Bresson's famous dictum.

As Cartier-Bresson writes, "Photography is the simultaneous recognition, in a fraction of a second, of the significance of an event as well as of a precise organization of forms which give that event its proper expression."[12] This well-known statement combines two of Cartier-Bresson's most useful insights for understanding Bhatt's work. First, the peculiar temporality of photography emerges from how its subjects unfold and vanish before the camera requires the photographer to be vigilant, for he "can never wind the scene backward in order to photograph it again".[13] And second, as Cartier-Bresson insists, "If a photograph is to communicate its subject in all its intensity, the relationship of form must be rigorously established."[14] In Bhatt's extraordinarily efficient post-1967 work there

3
Lost Pundit, by Jyoti Bhatt, 1965. Print
intaglio; composition: 66.5 x 46.2 cm,
sheet: 76 x 56.2 cm. Collection of Jyoti
Bhatt. Photograph: Jyoti Bhatt.

are decisive moments on every contact sheet, evidence of an adjusted attitude toward the
relationship between temporality, form, and content. One fairly straightforward example
of that is a photograph taken at the Santiniketan railway station in 1974, in which a
working-class man naps on the shaded shelf of a house-shaped ticket window, his body
surrounded by signboards in Roman and Bengali scripts. The image is formally arresting,
a play of shapes and scripts, not terribly different from *Lost Pundit*.[15]

The ideal of the decisive moment came to guide Bhatt's approach to the documentation
of folk art forms. One of his favourite photographs is of a woman whose body is echoed
by the peacock that sits on the roof of her house. It seems like the untitled photograph is
similar to *Lost Pundit* in its enjoyment of symbolic juxtaposition and the formal similarity
between the woman's body and the bird. The photograph from 1972 also documents the
practice of mandana, a floor- or wall-painting done in preparation for a festival or wedding.
From the late 1960s Bhatt began to survey practices of floor- and wall-paintings in multiple
regions of India, highlighting how pattern and symbolic meaning are foregrounded in the
complete absence of conceits of spatial depth. But the peacock photograph also captures
a fleeting moment, which is deepened by Bhatt's sense of his photography as a necessary
corrective to the effects of modernization on the vitality of folk art forms.

And yet, even as Bhatt's photographs evince a modernist anxiety about the vanishing
of culture, he describes a related sense of time inside folk art traditions, as well. As Bhatt

4
Tarnetar Fair, Saurashtra, 1959. Photograph by Jyoti Bhatt. Collection of Jyoti Bhatt.

5
N.S. Bendre sketching at Tarnetar Fair, Saurashtra, 1981. Photograph by Jyoti Bhatt. Collection of Jyoti Bhatt.

6
Tarnetar Fair, Saurashtra, 1959. Photograph by Jyoti Bhatt. Collection of Jyoti Bhatt.

7
Ticket Bari, West Bengal, 1974. Photograph by Jyoti Bhatt. Collection of Jyoti Bhatt.

writes, the peacock has symbolic importance in the tradition of mandana:[16] "In Rajasthan, where the presence of a peacock in the courtyard or on the rooftop is considered auspicious, the motif is understandably popular. *Perhaps it is to transform such fleeting moments into longer lasting ones, that peacock motifs are painted on the walls.*"[17] In other words, Bhatt captures a decisive moment in the sense valued by documentary photojournalism. But his photograph also explains this moment's decisiveness in terms of the woman's own situated knowledge, which is embedded in her painting practice.

Bhatt documented mandana at least five times, returning to villages in Rajasthan in 1972, 1976, 1981, 1985 and 1989. It was one of the few art practices that he studied in this longitudinal way. In our interview, Bhatt said he was attracted to the designs for their beauty, their boldness and intricacy, and their combination of symbolic meaning and individual improvisation. He also valued the process of the transmission of knowledge,

8
Woman making mandana, Rajasthan, 1972. Photograph by Jyoti Bhatt. Collection of Jyoti Bhatt.

and what that says about the passage of time. As he emphasizes, these women paint what is around them and what is passed down to them from their mothers and grandmothers, what they experience and what they know. And so mandana remains vital only as long as a way of life survives.

Bhatt had two major inspirations for his approach to collecting visual culture. The first was Subramanyan's idea of Indian visual culture as a system of visual communication, as a hierarchical language, where all forms were related, from the simplest to the most complex. Modern art sat at the head of this hierarchy, differentiated from folk art not only by its complexity, but by the critical stance taken by the artist. That is absent, Subramanyan argues, in folk art. Nilima Sheikh's notion of "good taste", cited earlier, is a riff on this idea of Subramanyan's. Her ironic tone places her among the Baroda artists who felt ambivalence about the relative hierarchical position held by modernism.

9
Woman making mandana, Rajasthan, 1976. Photograph by Jyoti Bhatt. Collection of Jyoti Bhatt.

In his 1992 article about Rajasthani mandana, Bhatt anticipates a common critique of folk art as lacking in individuality, in the sense of individual expression. While expression, as such, may not be valued by folk artists, he writes, practitioners can still easily identify individual artists' work. He describes folk artists as "improvising" and "reacting" to training, inspiration, and the work of their mothers and grandmothers. He implicitly questions what else might be meant by expression as it is used to describe modernist art. Also, although Bhatt does not overstate his case, he sees these works of art as agentive contributions to a system of folk knowledge.

Situated Knowledge in the Countryside
In our interviews, Bhatt cited the writings of Jhaverchand Meghani (1897–1947), a Gujarati nationalist, journalist, novelist and, crucially, documentarian, as his model for how to treat the situated knowledge embedded in folk practices. Meghani's novel, *Earthen Lamps* (*Mansai Na Diva*, published in 1946), begins with a journey.[18] The narrator walks with Ravishankar Maharaj, a brahmin Gandhian social worker who serves as his guide to the Mahi region of Gujarat. This was an unfamiliar place to Meghani, who was best known for his accounts of Saurashtra. Meghani presents his travels with Ravishankar as an education – in an appendix to the novel he calls it a "Mobile University" and goes so far as to recommend travel in the Gujarati countryside as a condition of graduation from the newly forming Gujarat University (p. 135). Ravishankar emphasizes the region's dangers, both social – it had reputation as a haven for "criminal tribes" – and natural (p. 1). From Mahi peasants, Ravishankar had learned that the Chitala plant's sap raises blisters; and the Antarvel vine, though beautiful, is a parasite – which Ravishankar compares to the British Raj (pp. 136–37).[19] Even the Mahi river was dangerous: a salt river whose "sole utility is that one can swear by its name" (p. 148). In a series of vignettes, Meghani presents the river as both a kind of wellspring of Mahi life and a metaphor for the situation of peasants,

10
Tarvani Fair, Saurashtra, 1977. Photograph by Jyoti Bhatt. Collection of Jyoti Bhatt.

who are squeezed between the tax "shark" and the vania moneylender, riven by caste and tribal conflicts, but most of all, enthralled by irrational superstitions.[20]

Meghani presents a conflict between two forms of knowledge, urban and rural, one that governs Jyoti Bhatt's approach to photography. Like Meghani, Bhatt does not treat Indian countryside as a "problem" to be solved through modernization, but as a source of wisdom that arises from constraint. One of his longest projects was on the rain festival undertaken by farmers in Brahmanwada in Gujarat in 1977.[21] Writing of this festival, which he describes as "a joyous … spectacle and a veritable theater of the street", Bhatt relates how this "superstition" arose as a "solution" to the problem of predicting long-term monsoon rainfall, a problem still unsolved by meteorology. He documents this festival as an artifact of indigenous knowledge. Its ultimate source is, as both Bhatt's photography and Meghani's writing contend, the land itself.

When I asked Bhatt to describe why he began to photograph the countryside, he talked mostly about the experience of travel itself. He emphasized the early difficulties he and his friends had travelling – they generally took their trips in June and because they had no vehicles, they walked between villages. In a favourite story, Bhatt recalls asking a passing man how far the next village was. The man pointed to his bidi and said, "About this far." Although tired from his long day's walk, Bhatt was immediately energized; clearly the village was very close

by. He and his friend quickened their steps. They walked ten miles, then twenty, but no village. Finally, long after dark, they reached the village and described what the man had told them. Was it a trick, they asked? Well, no. Everyone knows how you smoke a bidi: you light it, take a few drags, and when it goes out – as it always does – you put it behind your ear. You walk for a while, then light it again. It takes a long time to smoke a bidi. For Bhatt, travel was a pleasure, even when it wasn't.

It was also a duty. In a 2001 interview with me, Nilima Sheikh described a specifically Kathiawadi attachment to the landscape, common to those born in Saurashtra. Speaking as the wife of a Kathiawadi, Gulammohammed Sheikh, Nilima describes their curious preoccupation with the region: they feel beholden to it, facing duties pressed on them by the land itself. This indigenism is consonant with, but also goes beyond Subramanyan's directives. In Bhatt's stories, travel in Saurashtra is also a mode of rehabilitating the self, built first on the bodily challenges posed by travel in rural India at that time. Travel was a humbling, sometimes humiliating experience for Bhatt, who portrays himself as a more or less permanently callow urban youth. Bhatt consistently relates how he always expected to find kinship when he travelled in Saurashtra, but often was forced to face just how much he was separated from what he thought of as his homeland. In the very place where he sought to be rejuvenated, saved from the impoverishment of modern life, he was instead forced to acknowledge his own inability to connect. That's not just a modern view of travel, it's a modernist one. Aesthetic modernism, in India as in the West, has acknowledged alienation as fundamental to modernity, and found in travel a stage for the representation of that experience.

Subverting Hierarchical Distinctions

Form and content. Calculation and accident. Sign and meaning. Knowledge and superstition. A structuralist in practice, Jyoti Bhatt's work was organized by these binary distinctions, and his employment of them gave to his work a strongly analytical character. But he also consistently undermined the hierarchical distinction they implied, questioning to which pictorial element or form of truth each label should be applied. Nilima Sheikh suggests that Bhatt's analytical techniques were a product of his "modernist discernment", acquired through his modern education, including at the Faculty. But one can easily see Bhatt romantically rejecting this conclusion, insisting that the forms of knowledge he found outside of the city, as he travelled, were ultimately more formative of his work.

It is possible to see echoes of Bhatt's ambivalence about art hierarchies in the work of Baroda artists of his generation. This is as true of his mentor, K.G. Subramanyan, for whom the "living tradition" of non-modernist art was a source of immense power, as it is for artists who were his contemporaries, like Gulammohammed Sheikh.[22] For Sheikh, the art-historical past became as rich a source for alternative artistic values – whether they were narrative, illustration, or non-naturalistic treatments of space – as the countryside was for Bhatt.[23] Indeed, the same should be said for Nilima Sheikh herself, who shares Bhatt's interest in the relationship between image and text, though with wholly different results.[24]

What is particularly important about Bhatt's work, as an example of how modernism was practised in Baroda, is his disciplined yet playful interrogation of ideologies about art. That included both the expressive treatment of the artistic self, which Bhatt consistently mocked in his photographic self-portraits, and what was presented as the alternative, an investment in art's capacity to communicate meaning. Beyond the experimentation of the prints and the documentation of the photographs, which are of course both significant in themselves, Bhatt's practice is important as a staging of modernist aesthetic values. Of particular importance was the establishment of forms that contained historical, cultural and expressive content but could be implemented with a sense of critique and open-endedness. While much divided Baroda modernists in their pursuit of these forms, they shared a desire to subvert the hierarchical divisions that might be secreted within artistic practice.

11
Potter at work, Molela, Rajasthan, 1982. Photograph by Jyoti Bhatt. Collection of Jyoti Bhatt.

Notes

1   See, for example, William Archer, *India and Modern Art,* New York: Macmillan, 1959, and Suzi Gablik's review of Geeta Kapur's *Contemporary Indian Artists*, "The Disoriented Orient", *Times Literary Supplement*, November 10, 1978, p. 1304.

2   See Gulammohammed Sheikh, ed., *Contemporary Art in Baroda,* New Delhi: Tulika, 1997.

3   Group 1890 was a short-lived collective led by J. Swaminathan, who articulated the need to move beyond the terms in which Indian art was conceptualized in the 1950s. He viewed the work of art as the site of becoming, or the development of an authentic artistic subjectivity. See Rebecca M. Brown, "Group 1890 and the 1960s", in Partha Mitter, Parul Dave Mukherji and Rakhee Balaram, eds., *Twentieth Century Indian Art*, Milan: Skira, forthcoming.

4   See the essays by Amrita Gupta Singh and Shukla Sawant in Roobina Karode, ed., *Jyoti Bhatt: Parallels that Meet*, Delhi: Delhi Art Gallery, 2007.

5   I interviewed Jyoti Bhatt on a roughly biweekly basis while studying his photographs from November 2001 through February 2002 in Baroda. In the summer of 2002, I studied the related photographic surveys by photojournalist Bhupendra Karia and artist Raghav Kaneria.

6   Especially Karia, Kaneria, Kishor Parekh, and Raghu Rai.

7   Though it must be noted that Bhatt passed his matriculation in later years, after completing his art education at M.S. University, Baroda.

8   Nilima Sheikh, "A Post-Independence Initiative in Art", in Gulammohammed Sheikh, 1997, p. 85.

9   Ibid.

10   See interview with K.G. Subramanyan, *Lalit Kala Contemporary*, 18, c. 1972, pp. 25–28.

11   Jyoti Bhatt, personal communication, November 2001. Subramanyan enlisted his students and colleagues in Baroda in the collection of signs. Students and staff who pursued serious projects included Sankho Chaudhuri, Haku Shah, Raghav Kaneria, Suresh Sheth and Ushakant Mehta.

12   Henri Cartier-Bresson, *The Decisive Moment*, New York: Simon and Schuster, 1952, p. 42. Bhatt discusses his interest in Cartier-Bresson's work in his essay "Walls and Floors", in Karode, ed., 2007, p. 209.

13   Cartier-Bresson, 1952, p. 25.

14   Ibid., p. 32.

15   As Bhatt reports, his composition is deliberately ironic: the signs which read "Booking Window Open for 24 Hours" contrast sharply with the man napping on the window counter during the day.

16   Bhatt emphasizes how the photograph of the woman painting mandana peacocks also includes the bare wall of a pucca (concrete) house to the left. He observed that as soon as villagers are able to afford brick and mortar or stone houses, they no longer paint the walls, preferring to display their achievement of wealth.

17   Jyoti Bhatt, "Mandana: Wall and Floor Decorations", *India Magazine*, June 1992, p. 73. Emphasis in the original.

18   Jhaverchand Meghani, *Earthen Lamps*, translated by Vinod Meghani, New Delhi: Sahitya Akademi, 1979. Citations in the text have the relevant page numbers of this English edition.

19   Note the strong resonance of Meghani's narrative of local knowledge with Claude Levi-Strauss's "Science of the Concrete", in *The Savage Mind*, translated by John Weightman and Doreen Weightman, Chicago: University of Chicago Press, 1966.

20   See David Hardiman, *Feeding the Baniya: Peasants and Usurers in Western India*, Delhi: Oxford University Press, 1996.

21   Jyoti Bhatt, "And the Rains Came", *Swagat* (Indian Airlines in-flight magazine), July 1989, pp. 89–96.

22   K.G. Subramanyan, *The Living Tradition: Perspectives on Modern Indian Art*, Kolkata: Seagull Books, 1987; see also R. Sivakumar, ed., *K.G. Subramanyan: In Retrospect*, New Delhi: National Gallery of Modern Art, 2003; Geeta Kapur, *When Was Modernism: Essays in Contemporary Cultural Practice in India*, New Delhi: Tulika, 2000; and Gulammohammed Sheikh, 1997.

23   See Karin Zitzewitz, "Past Futures of Old Media: Gulammohammed Sheikh's *Kaavad: Travelling Shrine: Home*", in Arvind Rajagopal and Anupama Rao, eds., *Media & Utopia*, New Delhi: Routledge, forthcoming.

24   See Ananya Jahanara Kabir, *Territory of Desire: Representing the Valley of Kashmir*, Minneapolis: University of Minnesota Press, 2009, pp. 185–210.

Archival Imaginaries:
Art Practice and Pedagogy
in the Early Years of the FFA

Chithra K.S., Rashmimala Devi, Sabih Ahmed

In the year 1965 an application was sent from the M.S. University's Faculty of Fine Arts to the Vice Chancellor's office requesting approval of a budget to purchase books for an archive at the newly emerging art history department. Though classes on art history were a mainstay of the FFA since its inception in 1950, the Department of Art History and Aesthetics was officially established only in 1966. The request to the Vice Chancellor, however, was rather an odd one: the books purchased were to be regarded as consumables, just like chemicals in science laboratories. This did not sit easy with the university, since books were seen as permanent assets to be placed in a library rather than entities that vaporize. But after much persuasion the budget was approved, and the Department's archive was soon up and running. Art books and art magazines were purchased with immediate effect, in fact two copies of the same book in many cases, so that every coloured picture of art works in them could be cut and pasted onto cardboard "plates". The Department's archive flourished over the years, amassing more visual references and becoming a lively repository accessed constantly by students and teachers. No copy of that letter was to be found.[1]

Five decades on, archives today have a currency beyond our grasp. The very definition and parameters of the archive now expand so mercurially, it's difficult to measure the extent to which archives have become untethered from the fixity that state institutions and large infrastructures earlier commanded. And with ongoing technological developments, archiving stands today for a whole plethora of practices and forms. While traversing the broader discussions about archives, it is interesting to note that "The Archive" stands more like an allegory today in the face of a multitude of "archives" that have been manifest in different historical circumstances. Going beyond the archive as simply a collection of records, we are met with archive as place, archive as practice, archive as individual memory, and even archive as community.[2] More importantly, postcolonial discourses have paved the way for us to consider not merely the archival content and what it represents as much as the archival apparatus. And whereas in Europe there exists scholarship on archives, especially focused on the emergence of their modern construction that set the stage for the

Enlightenment, we are yet to see more of what an examination of archives in other parts of the world would offer. For one, the relationship between knowledge, power, resources (or the lack thereof), objects and belief systems in different contexts would shed light on very different issues and processes, at least so we should speculate. On the other hand, institutional archives within the colony (and particularly after decolonization) rarely came together to embody the integrity that "The Archive" technically suggests, be it in terms of either preservation standards or retrieval systems.

Tapati Guha-Thakurta's seminal book *Monuments, Objects, Histories: Institutions of Art in Colonial and Postcolonial India*[3] looks at various practices of representation such as photography, architectural drawing and plaster casting as being "constitutive of the depth and detail of a new field of knowledge" in the late 19th century, and thereby the formative years of (visual) documentation as being germane to the modelling of disciplines such as Art History and Archaeology in colonial India. Drawing from her work, this essay too comes with the conviction that archives constitute the practice and parameters of discourse, not just represent it. And it would be interesting to note how the canonizations of history that come of archival practice have shifted over time.

In this essay, we set out to examine the movement of one such archival imagination that arose in an art college established in the wake of a new nation. Whereas there is much to be said about changing relationships between art pedagogy and art practice at large, this essay will examine the first two decades of the institution's history, the consolidation of its visual art archive, and its correlation with a milieu that was cultivated in and around art-making.

Grounding Art Practice

With the establishment of the FFA, M.S. University of Baroda in 1950, a new moment for the visual arts was heralded, one where the "arts of the land could be reclaimed and freshly discerned; from which, with the birth of the modern nation, the adventure of modernism as initiated in the west could be experienced; and from which the artist could claim access to the art history of the world".[4] While precursors to, and the various trajectories that extended from, that moment are mapped elsewhere in this book, here, a closer attention to archival practices that developed in the college offers yet another interesting perspective over claims and contestations regarding modernity, the renewed interest and positioning of tradition, and the changing affinities between the region, nation and the world of art.

M.S. University was the first in the country to offer undergraduate degrees in the "fine arts". It distinguished itself from its immediate predecessor in Baroda – the polytechnic Kalabhavan that was set up in 1890, and deliberately departed from the colonial art school curricula emblematic of the Sir J.J. School of Art as well as from the revivalist slant prevalent in Santiniketan. Among the better known art schools of the time, the already available paradigms included the artisanal expertise that institutions like Kalabhavan propagated; the craftsmanship that colonial education sought to develop; the "Indian style" of painting taught at the Government School of Art in Calcutta;[5] and Santiniketan's locally rooted modernism that expanded into a Pan-Asian aesthetic. The intents and orientations in FFA's first decade suggest that it drew from these, but also chose a change of route. Though it needn't be overemphasized, a leaning towards art history and art theory was a crucial factor in setting new directions.

1
L.B. Shastri and V.K. Bhatt, Faculty of Fine Arts, M.S. University, 1959–60. Collection: Jyoti Bhatt.

It is telling that from the very beginning of the college in 1950, Markand Bhatt who was the first Dean and Head of the Applied Arts Department taught art history classes on modernism and "Western art", often using picture postcards of European art in his classes. B.N. Pancholi, also from the Applied Arts Department, took classes on the history of advertising, later joined by Vishnu Kumar Bhatt and L.B. Shastri in 1953 who took classes on the history of Indian art and Indian aesthetics as expounded in Sanskrit texts and canons. Among the teachers often remembered is V.R. Amberkar for his role in the foundation of art history and art theory classes in the college. Amberkar, though based in Bombay, would visit Baroda every few months and conduct classes in N.S. Bendre's home. It was he who introduced students to the likes of Heinrich Wolfflin and Benedetto Croce. But during the first few years, it is interesting to note that Western modernism was not taught via books, and there were reasons for this.

Markand Bhatt, while recalling his teaching in the FFA in the years 1950–59, wrote, "I also felt that as most of the students coming to the Faculty had a poor grasp of English and as the majority of them were from Gujarat, it would be helpful to them if the fundamentals of art, their use of plastic arts and the various concepts of aesthetics that I was endeavouring to teach them, were written in Gujarati with appropriate illustrative material. So after about five or six years of teaching experience from my 'instructional notes', with considerable strain and effort and with help from many students and colleagues, I wrote 'RUPAPRADAKALA'. The printing of the book took about two years and I published it in early 1958."[6] Bhatt acknowledges that detailed discussions and classification of elements of plastic arts that were provided in the book drew heavily from A.C. Barnes' *The Art in Painting*[7] and John Dewey's *Art as Experience*[8] along with other publications of the Barnes Foundation. There were also published references like the *Studio* magazine[9] from London, that was a constant source throughout the early years – Professor Mahendra Pandya recalls how as a student he first came across Barbara Hepworth's and Henry Moore's art works in this magazine, upon the urging of Professor Sankho Chaudhuri. Other magazines like *Domus*[10] (in Italian) and *L'Oiel*[11] (in French), were also favourites amongst students, as they had access to these in the library even if they couldn't read them.

However, drawing on sources of knowledge has always had multifarious avenues, never confined to references and citations found in publications and documents alone. The live studio demonstrations by, say, N.S. Bendre in cubist painting served almost as performative gestures of citation, where the artist's act of demonstrating captured the very experience and process of painting while referring to an art movement such as cubism.[12] Demonstrations were a practice prevalent in Santiniketan too, where the archival imagination relied on a different kind of visual aid. Parvez Kabir notes:

> [t]he project led by Nandalal Bose in Santiniketan is a prime example of this practice where images of the past were meant to be internalized [by copying and synthesizing their body image] and demonstrated on the grounds of formal enquiry. The Black house reliefs [pencil rubbings of reliefs], for example, were chosen by Nandalal precisely for demonstrative purposes, for example, the copy of a lion from a Mesopotamian relief served him as an example of alternative realism. In his book, "Vision and Creation", we find him arguing through this image on how different traditions found different logics behind the idea of *sadrsya*, or resemblance. However, it may be observed that it is only this formal logic through which objects from the past could enter into the art

2
N.S. Bendre in the Painting Studio, Faculty
of Fine Arts, M.S. University, 1959.
Collection: Jyoti Bhatt.

and art historical practice in Santiniketan. By contrast, enquiries into the past through archaeological or iconographic evidences remained relatively outside the ambit of art historical practices in Santiniketan and other art institutions.[13]

To say that Santiniketan and MSU's Faculty of Fine Arts stood for altogether different values surrounding archival imagination would be an exaggeration, but the research impetus in the FFA did have a distinct quality. The Santiniketan school relied largely on a mnemonics of performative internalization, while FFA moved increasingly in the direction of analytical examination and classification of art work images using physical documents and thus building an archival collection. The FFA eventually paved the way for discursive shifts in the art field, particularly towards a formalized, well-rounded art-education programme of a redefined cosmopolitanism that assimilated Western and non-Western references, modern and pre-modern discursive templates, and a renewed practice and theory relationship. An empirical and archival basis for art education was an important shift in the art field initiated by Baroda's Fine Arts Faculty. This ranged from live studio demonstrations, to sketching and conversing in-situ during study tours, to demonstration via slide-shows and plates, to building up a robust archive in the department. And all of these made the connection between art practice and citation from an archived art history inextricable.

(Re)Mapping Coordinates

> To: The Curator,
> Jalan Museum,
> Patna City
>
> Dear Sir,
> The Department of Art History at the Faculty of Fine Arts conducts courses in Indian, Western and Far-Eastern Art History at undergraduate and post-graduate levels and is building up an archive of visual material from the collection in India and Abroad. I have learnt of the Far Eastern collection of the Jalan museums[14] from several sources including Shri Benode Behari Mukherjee. We shall appreciate and gratefully acknowledge if you would kindly allow us to photograph your collection of Far Eastern Art and other relevant art objects. Shri Awanikant Deo who is a student of M.A. (Fine) in painting is authorised to photograph there [sic] objects. Thank you in anticipation.
> Sincerely
> (Gulam Mohammed Sheikh)
> Lecturer in Art History and Aesthetics

This letter, dated May 11, 1978,[15] lays out a number of interesting cues as to what was going on at the FFA towards archive-building almost three decades after its establishment. For one, the geographic coordinates of the art history courses were well in place – Indian, Western, Far-Eastern. Second, the expansion of the Department's archival collection was being conducted in a concerted and planned manner to go hand-in-hand with the courses taught. And third, the process of documentation was being carried out even by students who practised art-making, thereby not confining the effort of archive-building to the Art History Department alone.

During conversations with artists who had been students of the FFA in the first two decades,[16] it was interesting to learn that this practice of gathering references and documenting art objects and monuments (either by taking pictures or collecting magazines) was already widespread. An impetus for art practice to partake of a newly envisaged (art) history? Perhaps so, if we are allowed to maintain that modern art as a field[17] was as much defining itself by charting its historical lineages as it was by situating its persuasions in the contemporary moment. And likewise, differences too were being established so as to distinguish modern art from, say, theatre, design and crafts, which immediately after Independence were in the process of institutionalizing themselves (or being institutionalized in the case of crafts) via their own distinguished legacies.[18] While the modern visual artist would draw enormously from the vast reserve of tradition in art and other fields, it was equally critical for the visual artist to distinguish his or her work from those other domains.

Coming to the question of contemporaneous affinities, it goes without saying that after World War II, and especially by the 1960s, global networks and flows of knowledge and power were already realigned creating different compulsions for geo-political allegiances.[19] The Faculty was not insulated from any of these; on the contrary, it was very much in the thick of them. Besides the well-known fact that Markand Bhatt brought his exposure at the Barnes Foundation with him, Sankho Chaudhuri had already been on a study tour of Europe.[20] Bendre had visited China and Japan, and in 1962 he had participated in the

Conference of International Association of the Plastic Arts in New York. K.G. Subramanyan had studied at Slade School of Art in London (1955–56) on a British Council Research Scholarship.[21] Jeram Patel had completed a diploma in 1959 from the Central School of Arts and Crafts, London, where he studied Typography and Publicity Design, before he began teaching at the Faculty. Among the immediately following generation of artists who studied under them in Baroda, Jyoti Bhatt went on to study printmaking at Pratt Institute and Pratt Graphic Art Center, New York, on a Fulbright scholarship and John D. Rockefeller 3rd grant between 1964 and 1966.[22] Ratan Parimoo was a recipient of the Commonwealth Scholarship to study History of Art at Courtauld, London, between 1960 and 1963. Gulammohammed Sheikh, a well regarded poet in Gujarati by the late 1950s, also received the Commonwealth Scholarship and studied at the Royal College of Art between 1963 and 1966. Mahendra Pandya received a British Council grant to study methodology of teaching sculpture and to visit sculptors' studios in 1965. *Art Now in India*, curated by George Butcher for the Commonwealth Arts Festival in London in 1965, had works by N.S. Bendre, Bhupen Khakhar, and Himmat Shah. A deeper and longer connection between the FFA and London was imminent, shifting the focus away from the Parisian slant that had seemed to characterize the formidable Bombay Progressives. But that's another story.

Alongside the centrifugal strands that spread into a newly aligning art world, there was an equally strong centripetal curve towards the indigenous arts and crafts of the country amongst teachers and students in the college. In 1953, the *First All India Handicrafts Board's Exhibition* was organized by Sankho Chaudhuri. In 1958, K.G. Subramanyan moved to Bombay as Deputy Director (Designs) at the Weavers' Service Centre of the All India Handloom Board, finally returning to Baroda in 1961 as Reader in the Painting Department while continuing to work with the All India Handloom Board as a consultant. Traditional artists had a prominent presence in the Faculty, such as Puna Khima Kumbhar who taught pottery and Gyarsilal Varma[23] who was Demonstrator in Mural Techniques from the mid-1950s.

Such exposure and affinities among other reasons had longstanding repercussions in the general outlook towards art practice and art history among the art community coming together in Baroda. The frames of reference, as would be obvious, were entirely different from any of the FFA's predecessors among art colleges in the country; here, assimilating traditional techniques and being trained in fine arts practice were imbricated with learning and developing art history. The archival impulses seemed to be a crucial aspect in this. It is worth taking note of the fact that documentation was even initiated independently of the institution by artists at the time, Jyoti Bhatt's commitment to photo-documenting the living traditions of India being most noteworthy.[24] Other artists too were committed to such a calling, among them Raghav Kaneria who was directly associated with Jyoti Bhatt. There were more projects in the subsequent years too, such as Nilima Sheikh's research and documentation of the pichhwais of Nathdwara in 1986–87. It would not be far-fetched to say that there was a kind of self-reflexivity among artists (and students) about the interconnectedness of pedagogy, historical acuity and contemporary aspirations, as is demonstrated in an essay Gulammohammed Sheikh wrote in 1978 where he suggested about his contemporaries that "the new artist freely and guiltlessly draws from all available sources – Indian and Western, traditional and modern … [and a] growing involvement with the local environment, its shift from generalities to specific areas of interest."[25] Art was indeed an act of drawing from and drawing towards different ways to look at history.

The Archive Manifest

When in 1966 the Department of Art History and Aesthetics was formally established, Ratan Parimoo led the determined enterprise of collecting reproductions and documentation for the Department's archive. This might perhaps have been the first endeavour of its kind in an institute of art education in the country, where a comprehensive collection of art work images was amassed and classified in close association with curriculum-building. The circumstances and resources were dismal, the methods exceptional. As mentioned earlier in this essay, books were dismembered to create plates, students and teachers took it upon themselves to photo-document in museums and at historical sites, slides and photographs were collected from wherever possible, there was even an appeal to contemporary artists to send in details of their life and work for inclusion in the archive.

Parimoo remembers Zimmer's book[26] being the first that was purchased in order for its images to be cut out and pasted on pieces of cardboard, which would in turn be arranged in different boxes classified by category. And among European artists, Van Gogh had the first box dedicated to him, with around 50 pictures of his paintings mounted on those cardboard "plates". Parimoo had first witnessed this process of plucking images from publications in the Courtauld Institute where a similar procedure was applied to books on Russian art because of the inaccessibility of other sources at the time. In a letter written in October 1974 to the M.S. University Vice Chancellor regarding the appointment of an Archivist in the Department, Parimoo had stated that the archival collection had grown to over 8,000 slides and over 10,000 photographs and reproductions.[27]

The act of destroying books for the purpose of archive-building holds much importance since it established a new form of material to study with and shifted the pedagogic practices of fine arts considerably. Since the Art History Department's archive was firmly embedded in teaching, it established a rather new relationship between art pedagogy and image referencing. As much as students until then were used to encountering images of art works in books, where they were carefully placed in a historical and chronological perspective (either by the epoch that the art works belonged to, or the style and medium they were illustrative of, or the art movements they came out of), the archive untethered them in a manner of speaking. Much in the way we are used to finding discrete references on digital platforms, the Department's archive paved the way to flexibly navigate and juxtapose images for analytical (and playful) comparative exercises. There was of course some classification of images that continued to be promulgated by lectures and examinations. This is a point that has been elaborated on earlier by Parvez Kabir who writes:

> The act of showing images from books while giving a lecture still had its roots in the practice of demonstration, and it invariably lacked the fluidity of handling separate images. Images from books are still considered "plates" and much like "templates" they had a strong indexical quality, like messages arranged in order ... however large the numbers of images are, the viewer's orientation is always controlled and governed by the very form of the book itself. With time it always happens that the material in the form of a book shapes a lecture more than the lecture which is supposed to shape its materials. The image archive freed its images from such limitations; plucked, separated and collected as "images in themselves".[28]

The Art History Department's archive contained a number of other kinds of objects for reference purposes, such as 35mm slides that were projected during lectures, plaster-cast

DEPARTMENT OF ART HISTORY & AESTHETICS
FACULTY OF FINE ARTS
M.S.UNIVERSITY OF BARODA
BARODA-2
28th Dec.'1966.
(First issued on 10th Jan'1964.)

Dear Shri/ Smt.

We have started a programme of collecting information on contemporary
Indian artists. This includes details about their life and work.
Eventually it will take the shape of an archive housing photographs,
prints and original works and writings by and on the artists where
also all the biographical material on them will be collected.

For this purpose we would like a year by year account of you from
your birth till today including the institutions where you have had
your education and training, details about your one-man-shows and
exhibitions in which you have participated, countries you have visited
and the impact they have had on you, names of museums and private
collectors who have bought your works, your activities like execution
of commissions or as a teacher of art, your other interests and
hobbies. Finally a statement of your own ideas which may include
mention of those artists or personalities (or books) whose work and
ideas you appreciate most and who may have inspired you. We would also
like to know your estimation of Indian art of today and of World art
in general and what role a young painter in this country can play in
the present situation. Of particular interest would be to know your
observations on your own development as an artist, the stages through
which you have passed and some comments on those of your works which
you consider significant and representing various stages of your
development. In this connection any letters addressed by you or to you
bearing on your ideas as an artist may be brought to our notice. So
also typed copies of reviews of your work and interviews taken may
be conveyed to us. Much useful would be a bibliography listing all
those articles on you (or by you) which may have appeared in news-
papers, magazines and books including names of authors and dates.
Lastly we shall much appreciate if you could send us catalogues of
your previous exhibitions, photographs and colour reproductions of
your work and possibly also original sketches,drawings or graphic
prints.Special care will be taken to preserve all this material and
documents in our library.

This may be taken as a permanent request to you so that of and
on you would keep us sending various kinds of information and material
regarding your work including notices and catalogues of your subsequent
one -man-shows. You may also deposit with us any other information or
material or letters regarding yourself or other artists in your
possession that you consider fit to be recorded for posterity.

There is a great need for a systematic and authoritative study of
contemporary Indian art. It is the information supplied by you which
will enable us to prepare such a study for which your co-operation
is earnestly solicited. In the past, arts in this country went into
oblivion partly also due to the lack of contemporaneous chroniclers
or critics who could have recorded lives and activities of artists
of the time. It is our sincere hope that such a situation shall not
repeat.

The amount of information and documents assembled with the help of
your co-operation could be unique and probably would make the only
reference library of its kind in the country. It may also form an
indispensable archive which will be useful for all research workers
on the twentieth century Indian art.

We request once again your active response and full co-operation.

                                        Yours faithfully,

                                        Ratan Parimoo.
                                        Head,Deptt.of Art History
Kcm/*28.12.66.   *****   & Aesthetics.

3
Letter from Ratan Parimoo, December 28, 1966, sent to artists requesting their contribution to the Department's archive. From the digital collection of the Ratan Parimoo Archive as part of The Baroda Archives project, Asia Art Archive. Collection: Ratan Parimoo.

4
During the University Grants Commission (UGC) National Seminar (on site), *Ellora Caves: Sculptures and Architecture*, Department of Art History and Aesthetics, M.S. University, 1985 (proceedings published in 1988). Collection: Ratan Parimoo.

reproductions of pre-modern Indian and non-Indian sculptures in the foyer, scrapbooks of newspaper clippings and even a small collection of original paintings.[29] Yet, the overall impact of the archive was felt most effectively in how it allowed the discipline of art history to visibly depart from fields like archaeology and Indology, in favour of stylistic analyses, iconography and multiple lines of enquiry. This departure was ostensibly articulated by Parimoo himself, two decades after the Department was established, when he wrote to Kapila Vatsyayan, stating that "[a]fter having taught all these years and having worked with Sanskritists, Archaeologists, Historians and Philosophers, I feel convinced strongly that Departments of Art History must have specialists in Art History. Otherwise we will never have art historical scholarship beyond the typical Department of Ancient Indian History, Culture, Archaeology, etc."[30]

We may like to view this as a process where a discipline's own formation was firmly tied to establishing its own archive. In hindsight, it becomes apparent that in this reciprocal relationship between the building up of the Department's archive and the way art history as a discipline was being configured, certain parameters of what lay in the fold of art history and what did not were also being configured. A leaning towards prevailing notions of classical Indian arts and architecture was visible, as was that towards European Renaissance, and towards the major art movements of the 20th century in India, Europe and America. However, despite the fact of a pervasive interest amongst the Baroda artist community in the traditional arts and crafts of India, the Department archive (and curriculum) seems not to have reflected this.[31] However, the point of mentioning this is less to enquire about an inclusion-exclusion debate, but rather to signal that there is much research yet to be done about how a variety of art practices were discursively framed, what institutional manifestations they took, and in what ways discourse (and individual effort) organized itself in relation to such institutional manifestations.

It may be safe to say that in a project of disciplining the archive in the FFA, a formalistic credence in approaching art was inadvertently reinforced. Furthermore, perhaps this

5
Professor Ratan Parimoo (seated) and
sculptor Mahendra Pandya, during the
University Grants Commission (UGC)
International Seminar on *The Art of Ajanta
and Its Significance in Asian Art*, held at the
Department of Art History and Aesthetics,
M.S. University, 1988. Collection: Ratan
Parimoo.

can be seen as aligned with the proclivity that artists had towards citing from eclectic
sources, quoting from traditions and art works across history, and reimagining the
tableaux of historical representation. And in taking this line of thought, we may say that
Baroda's pedagogy that began as an experiment led to artists and art historians creating
an epistemological means to redraw (and rewrite) art-historical lineages afresh and even
figure themselves in them. The emphasis of Figuration and Narrativizing, then, can perhaps
connote a different meaning, one of artists constantly experimenting with representative
means to position and reposition themselves in art history at each given present.

   This essay has been an attempt to examine a small portion of the history of modern
art, seen through the prism of its institutionalization. In taking pedagogic institutions to
be one among other agents of modernity, a closer look at the early years of an institution
such as the FFA offers an interesting insight into ways in which the art community was
grappling with modernity, tradition, contemporaneity, and its own position in being an
agent in history. While this is only a preliminary study, the proximity between pedagogy
and historical and archival impulses on the one hand, and artistic practice on the other,
seems apparent in how crucial they were in constituting modern art's discourse and testing
its parameters for a generation of artists and in decades to follow. In a way, the object of
this essay has been to understand that active engagement by the art community in their
attempt to assemble and reassemble the material history is made of.[32]

Notes

1   As recounted by Ratan Parimoo in an interview with the authors on January 12, 2013.

2   Andrew Flinn, "Community Histories, Community Archives: Some Opportunities and
    Challenges", *Journal of the Society of Archivists*, Vol. 28, No. 2, October 2007.

3   Tapati Guha-Thakurta, *Monuments, Objects, Histories: Institutions of Art in Colonial and
    Postcolonial India*, New York, New Delhi: Columbia University Press, Permanent Black, 2004.

4   Nilima Sheikh, "A Post-Independence Initiative in Art", in Gulammohammed Sheikh, ed., *Contemporary Art in Baroda*, New Delhi: Tulika, 1997, p. 55.

5   Tapati Guha-Thakurta, "Abanindranath, Known and Unknown: The Artist versus the Art of His Times", in Gayatri Sinha, ed., *Art and Visual Culture in India: 1857–2007*, Bombay: Marg Publications, 2009.

6   Markand Bhatt's letter to Gulammohammed Sheikh, January 8, 1987. From the digital collection of the Gulammohammed Sheikh Archive as part of The Baroda Archives project, Asia Art Archive.

7   A.C. Barnes, *The Art in Painting*, New York: Harcourt, Brace & World, Inc., 3rd ed., 1937.

8   John Dewey, *Art as Experience*, New York: Perigee Trade, 1934.

9   *The Studio: an illustrated magazine of fine and applied art*, an illustrated fine arts and decorative arts magazine published in London from 1893 until 1964.

10 *Domus* had been founded in Italy in 1928 as an architecture and design magazine. After the Second World War its founder Gio Ponti had returned as editor after a seven-year hiatus, bringing the magazine into the forefront of contemporary international debates and artistic trends.

11 *L'Oeil* was a French magazine about contemporary art founded in 1955 by Rosamond Bernier and Georges Bernier.

12 M.F. Husain, K.H. Ara, M.R. Achrekar, K.K. Hebbar and Ram Kinker Baij were among the many artists who had visited the Faculty in the 1950s and '60s and offered studio demonstrations to students.

13 Parvez Kabir, *An Archive Remembered: Presenting the Image Archive of the Art History Department, Faculty of Fine Arts, The Maharaja Sayajirao University of Baroda*, published in Asia Art Archive's "DIAAALOGUE", April 2011 (www.aaa.org.hk).
    It must also be noted that field trips to archaeological sites and historical monuments were an integral part of the programme in the FFA. These "study tours", as they continue to be referred to, included visits to Badami, Pattadakal, Konark, Ajanta and Ellora among other sites.

14 The Jalan Museum is a private museum in Patna. It was founded in 1919 by the late R.K. Jalan, a collector.

15 From the digital collection of the Gulammohammed Sheikh Archive as part of The Baroda Archives project, Asia Art Archive.

16 From 2012 to 2014, the authors of this essay have been in conversation with a number of artists in Baroda as part of the research for The Baroda Archives project of the Asia Art Archive. The artists include Jyoti Bhatt and Jyotsna Bhatt, Naina Dalal, Mahendra Pandya, Narendra Sant, Nilima Sheikh, Gulammohammed Sheikh and Ratan Parimoo among others.

17 At least in its institutionalization via pedagogy, museums and critical discourse.

18 It must be noted how crucial the institutions were in determining the conditions of artistic production, from influencing artistic aspirations, to representing artists in exhibitions and playing the role of patrons. Comparative research across institutions as they developed in the early decades after Independence would be compelling in this regard to say the least; including, for example, the National School of Drama (1959), the Film Institute in Pune (1960), the National Handicrafts and Handlooms Museum (1956), the National Gallery of Modern Art (1954) and the Lalit Kala Akademi (1954).

19 A closer reading of how American patronage and cultural policies contributed to a new geography of contemporary art in India can be found in Christine Ithurbide's "Shaping a Contemporary Art Scene: The Development of Artistic Circulation, Networks, and Cultural Politics between India and the U.S. since 1950s", http://www.rockarch.org/publications/resrep/ithurbide.pdf.

20 Having worked in Paris and England in 1949, Chaudhuri had visited Italy, Switzerland, Belgium and Holland around the same time. In 1961, he was part of the *International Symposium of Sculptors* in Yugoslavia. In 1965, he had even toured Russia as a guest of the Artists Union.

21 In a conversation with the authors, Subramanyan recalled that it was during this time that he came into contact with Henry Moore and Victor Pasmore.

22 By then, he had already studied painting and etching at Academia Di Belle Arti in Naples under an Italian Government scholarship.

23 More on Gyarsilal Varma can be read in Nilima Sheikh, 1997, p. 128.

24 For around three decades beginning in 1967, and using his own means, Bhatt took on the project of travelling to numerous villages in India to photograph artisan communities and the process of their art-making, finally amassing over 30,000 photographs chronologically organized with copious notes in his diaries about the contexts and changing techniques and mediums of their practice. For further discussions on Bhatt's documentation projects see Karin Zitzewitz in this volume.

25 Gulammohammed Sheikh, "New Contemporaries", *Glimpses of Wonder and Beauty: Indian Heritage*, Bombay: Marg Publications and Indian Society for Art Appreciation, 1978.

26 Heinrich Zimmer, *The Art of Indian Asia*, New York: Pantheon Books, 1955.

27 Ratan Parimoo's letter to the Vice Chancellor, M.S. University, October 29, 1974. From the digital collection of the Ratan Parimoo Archive as part of The Baroda Archives project, Asia Art Archive.

28 Kabir, 2011.

29 A detailed account of these is offered in Kabir's 2011 paper.

30 Letter written by Ratan Parimoo (then Professor and Head of the Art History and Aesthetics Department) to Kapila Vatsyayan (then Additional Secretary in the Ministry of Education, New Delhi), on July 5, 1984. From the digital collection of the Ratan Parimoo Archive as part of The Baroda Archives project, Asia Art Archive.

31 Though it is necessary to mention here that attempts were made by Gulammohammed Sheikh to introduce a course on "Living Tradition of Indian Art" in 1987 after a series of workshops in the Department of Painting between 1984 and 1986 on patachitra scrolls, kalamkari, weaving in pitlooms etc. A proposal for this course is in the digital collection of the Gulammohammed Sheikh Archive as part of The Baroda Archives project, Asia Art Archive. Nor can we forget that Subramanyan, Parimoo and Sheikh themselves were thoroughly preoccupied in their own ways with questions of tradition, folk arts and craft, and indigenous cultures.

32 The authors have been involved in The Baroda Archives project that was initiated by Asia Art Archive in November 2011. This is a digitization project comprising 40,000+ scanned and annotated documents that make up the personal collections of Jyoti Bhatt, Ratan Parimoo, Gulammohammed Sheikh and K.G. Subramanyan – all four artists and at various times influential teachers in the FFA. The project brings to light the role that art schools played in shaping the field of visual arts in postcolonial India when pedagogy and experimentation coalesced to think about art anew. These archives are now available online at http://www.aaa.org.hk/Collection/SpecialCollections/Details/37.

City as Metaphor: An Archaeology of Contemporary Artistic Production and Display

Santhosh S.

> One only knows a spot once one has experienced it in as many dimensions as possible. You have to have approached a place from all four cardinal points if you want to take it in, and what's more, you also have to have left it from all these points. Otherwise it will quite unexpectedly cross your path three or four times before you are prepared to discover it.
>
> – Walter Benjamin, *Moscow Diary*

It is well known that Baroda as a site stands for what is considered a distinctive modernist phase within the larger narrative of artistic production in India post-Independence. This fact, coupled with Baroda's historical legacies and its pivotal role in the shaping of art education and contemporary art practices in the country has been well documented and critically evaluated in the book *Contemporary Art in Baroda*, edited by one of the torchbearers of the city's cultural legacy, Professor Gulammohammed Sheikh.[1] This essay takes cues from Sheikh's significant initiative, but its mandate is not predicated upon an extension of the latter's arguments. On the one hand, the essay attempts to capture the dynamics of a decade following the publication of Sheikh's book on Baroda. But on the other, it prefers to approach this place – following Benjamin[2] – from "all four cardinal points" and to leave it "from all these points", like a flaneur, whose endless walks in the city produce a cohabitating but fractured and layered picture of it.[3]

Whenever I think of Baroda as a city as well as a site of artistic production and display, it appears as a metaphor for exteriority. As an imaginary space, it tangentially evokes zones of utopia. Like many other provenances, it too claims to inhabit distinct interiorities. These aspects definitely have markers of truth-effects of their own. However, this essay puts forth the proposition that, more than the stigmata of internal truth, the sores of these exteriorities are central in understanding the web of complexities through which artistic production, display, dissemination and consumption are organized within the body-politics of the city. To that end, the attempt here is not merely to engage with the historical legacy of the cosmopolitan culture of the city but to critically examine the lived reality of this notion within the Faculty of Fine Arts and the neighbouring cityscape, particularly between 1997 and 2007. In a way, such a framework may allow us to engage with the problematics involved in categorically attributing cosmopolitanism as the ethical genesis of the provenance.

Cosmopolitan Inheritance and "The Secular Lies of Baroda"

As renowned journalist Sankarshan Thakur noted in 2006, in the context of the overnight demolition of a roadside Sufi shrine by the Vadodara Municipal Corporation[4] and the ensuing violence, "Old Baroda isn't a town; it's an eruption of seething frontiers mined with malevolence. Prejudice, hatred, anger, suspicion, distrust, vile and vicious myth ...."[5] This observation registers the fact that beneath the surface realities of cosmopolitanism, Baroda also bears deep wounds of communalism. Professor J.S. Bandukwala, a prominent public intellectual and professor of Physics at M.S. University is quoted in Thakur's essay as saying that "Our lives [in Baroda] are not stretches of normality interrupted by violence, they are stretches of violence interrupted by normality. At least two generations have no memory of peace or harmonious living. Mayhem is normal."[6]

These despairing remarks about Baroda work as a signpost for me to revisit some of the experiential realities which haunt me even today. I remember how, as students at the FFA (I joined in 1999), we were warned not to venture into the old city area because of communal riots. What repeatedly took me by surprise was the casualness with which these messages were imparted – the lack of any emotional content, any humanitarian or political concern in them, as if this violence was taking place on another continent.

Walling the City

Such backdrops also need to be taken into account when dealing with the contemporary history of Baroda/Vadodara. And within this context, we would unarguably need to direct our attention to the genocidal violence in Gujarat unleashed by majoritarian forces in 2002 against the Muslim minority, and its impact on this provenance. The 2002 violence exposed the ugly reality behind the city's cosmopolitan facade. The routine riots which were otherwise quarantined within the confines of the "old city", and had been regarded as "remote information" for the cosmopolitan "new city", were all at once transformed into a nightmare-come-true for both liberals and critics of liberalism alike.

The scale and intensity of this violence had an immediate impact on most artists. It certainly was an eye-opener for many. For instance, as a response, the exhibition *Voices against Violence* was organized in October 2002 at the Exhibition Hall of the FFA, with a large number of artists participating.[7] In fact, the annual examination display of students' works in May 2002 itself saw some immediate responses to the horrific effects they experienced during this period. But in both instances, most responses were more of an outburst of emotion than products of any concrete engagement with questions of majoritarianism and its local manifestations. And needless to say, once "normalcy" had been re-established, Baroda's artist community returned to its "burrows of comfort".

This aspect of exteriority – of distancing and externalizing the most proximal and the intense – has wider implications for cultural practice at large. The spatial divides (including that of the mental-scape) construct their own zones of exclusivity in relation to cultural practices. In other words, the realm of culture is ascribed to the spatial configuration of the new by othering the old into the imaginary space of social neurosis. This is evident in the reluctance of many politically committed art practitioners to engage with the particularities of lived reality (and of violence); most of them would rather wilfully concern themselves with universal notions of human suffering. It is important to note that such abstract universality is central to the production of a formal cosmopolitan culture. And such

1
Old City: Leharipura Gate, 2012.

2
New City: 7 SEAS Mall, Fatehgunj, 2011.

3 & 4
Voices against Violence: Artists against
Communalism exhibition organized by
Vadodara Shanti Abhiyan, Sahaj and
Citizens' Confluence. FFA Gallery, October
2–6, 2002. Photographs: Indrapramit Roy.

5
City for Sale, by Gulammohammed Sheikh, 1981–84. Oil on canvas, 223.5 x 305.2 cm. Courtesy of the Trustees of the Victoria and Albert Museum, London.

formal universalization loses its "formalism" once it is understood that the production and exclusion of the concrete is a necessary precondition for the very fabrication of the formal.

This is not to say that there are no instances of artistic involvement with questions of majoritarianism, its local manifestations and the traumatic effects of violence. One such early, significant instance can be traced back to the works of Gulammohammed Sheikh.[8] Another citable example is B.V. Suresh's series of works based on the 2002 genocide, executed in various mediums and media.[9] Suresh's engagement with the specificities of violence (such as the use of burnt bread loafs in one of the installations – a reference to the infamous Best Bakery massacre)[10] is in fact a significant artistic intervention where the *particular* re-stores its potential to stand-in for the *universal* without losing its local specificity. A third instance, in a different register, is Vasudha Thozhur's longstanding association with riot-affected citizens in creative curative programmes, with resonances of these experiences being apparent in her own artistic production.[11]

However, such references, of which there may be others, designate distinct individual approaches; at a broader level, there is hardly any evidence to suggest that artists as a "linguistic community", especially in the context of Baroda, engaged with these questions in any substantive and collective manner. This is evident in the fact that there have hardly been any attempts at initiating new modes of collaborative practices, community-based or public art projects from artistic or pedagogical points of view. Such forays could have enabled FFA as an institution to connect with the neighbouring communities. On the contrary, FFA was self-fashioned through the notion of the lone artistic figure, and idealized its isolated existence (even within the University community) as part of its cultivated ethos.[12] Keeping in mind these specific trajectories, we need to locate artistic practices in Baroda within the larger field of artistic production. Hence, it is important to revisit some of the drastic shifts in national economic policy in recent decades, and their impact on the field.

6

Retakes of the Shadows, a part of *Facilitating the Beast*, by B.V. Suresh, 2006. Installation with burnt bread loaves and video projection, alluding to the Best Bakery Case, Gujarat, 2002. Collection: B.V. Suresh. Photograph: B.V. Suresh.

7

Beyond Pain: An Afterlife (2013), by Vasudha Thozur in collaboration with Himmat, a women's collective formed by those widowed in Naroda Patiya in 2002. (Right) *Anatomy of Celebration* by Vasudha Thozur; (left) individual works by young victims. Courtesy Sakshi Gallery and Project 88, Mumbai.

8
Digital Art Demonstration at ART Underground, 2001. (Left to right) Asokan Poduval, Hina Bhatt, Kavita Shah, Vinod Shah and a visitor. Collection: Nandini and Amitabh Gandhi. Photograph: Raju Kahar; digital copying: Manish Chauhan.

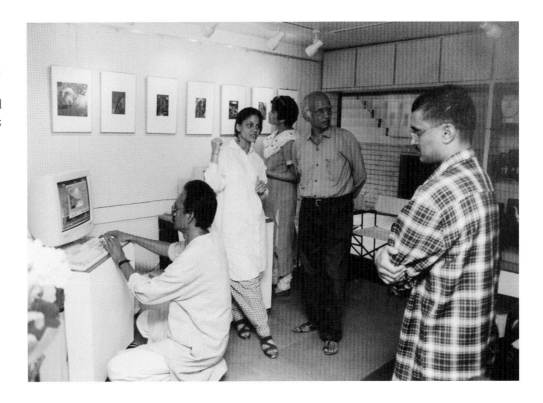

The Story of Capital Inflow

The dominance of commercial art galleries, which coincided with the unprecedented capital inflow into the art market, deserves close attention. As we know, these developments were a by-product of the liberalization policies unleashed since the early 1990s, which in turn completely transformed the character of the Indian economy – from mixed to market economy. Concurrent with these developments in the economy were similar developments in the field of cultural production. This resurgence of the market economy provided many artists with great exposure. In parallel, a new league of buyers and international networks of marketing Indian art emerged.[13]

During this period, Baroda too witnessed the establishment of a number of commercial art galleries.[14] One of the notable ventures was the establishment in 2003 of the ABS Gallery (later renamed ABS Lanxess, and later still, Red Earth Gallery), which to date is the most equipped and spacious of private/corporate-owned galleries in Baroda. It organized many group as well as solo exhibitions but hardly hosted any exhibitions that put the gallery on the national or international map. Notable here is also the presence of a relatively small and short-lived gallery, ART Underground, which is one of the earliest galleries (in India) to focus on supporting and promoting new media art practices.[15]

The mushrooming of private galleries in most metropolitan centres across India was an outcome of economic liberalization, and similar tendencies in Baroda can also be seen through this light. At the same time, it is important to note that unlike metropolises such as Mumbai or Delhi, most galleries in Baroda never emerged as major players in the national or global art market. In fact, they largely worked as suppliers of art works for individual buyers within the city or as satellite centres for galleries in other metropolises. This aspect is further indicative of the fact that even during the time of the great art market "boom" (of the early 2000s), Baroda largely remained known as a major centre for artistic production rather than for exhibition or as an independent centre of economic transactions. Some of the related outcomes of these developments can be seen in the proliferation of various studio spaces and the organization of numerous artists' camps.

The Poetic Spaces of Patronage

Initiatives such as the establishment of artist studio spaces in Baroda, beginning in the early 2000s, have already had considerable impact on artistic practices in the city. These artist studios have been established by various patrons of art – sometimes gallerists, sometimes corporate patrons, and in a few cases by artists themselves. Two early initiatives by gallerists and corporate patrons were Priyasri Artist Studio (2004) and Space Studio (2005). Space Studio, for instance, was formerly an industrial warehouse, and accommodates over a dozen artists at any given point of time. It provides independent studio spaces at no rental cost for upcoming artists, particularly those who have recently completed their Fine Arts education.

9
Space Studio, 2014.

10
Chhaap, old premises at Karelibaug, 1999.
(Left to right) Gulammohammed Sheikh,
Rekha Rodwittiya, B.V. Suresh, Vasudevan
Akkitham, Bhupen Khakhar, Jeram Patel.
Photograph: Atul Garg, courtesy Kavita
Shah.

11
Chhaap, new premises at Old Padra Road,
2014. Kavita Shah with Vijay Bagodi and
Kurma Nadham.

In more than one way, Space and other such studios have provided a platform for these artists, both by facilitating greater interactive possibilities among artists working in these studio spaces and by functioning as a mediator between gallery owners, art enthusiasts and artists, thereby becoming a quasi-exhibitionary space for resident artists.

However, it is equally important to examine some of the structural limitations of these initiatives and critically scrutinize their economic dimension. To begin with, the criteria for selection of artists in these studio spaces are largely arbitrary in nature and very often only based on the "tastes" of the patron. As such, while there may be no economic transactions based on the exchange of modern currency involved (since the studios are free of rental charges), artists provided with the opportunity to work in any of these spaces are obliged to "gift" some of their works to the studio (again, based on the tastes of the patron) during the course of their residency.[16] This unequivocal right of the patron to select works to be kept can perhaps hamper the cooperative ethos of such initiatives. In that sense, even though such studio spaces are projected as "artist cooperatives", one should consider these initiatives not merely as philanthropic ventures or acts of patronage, but also as new business models that emerged during this time, since the aspect of economic capital is central to their organization. An exceptional instance of merit that deserves special mention here is the establishment of the non-profit initiative, Chhaap, which was set up in order to encourage printmaking practices.[17]

Another economic model that emerged in a big way during this period is that of the artists' camp. Here, generally, patrons organize camps in tourist or exotic locations (sometimes even in hotels in metropolitan cities) for a span of 5–15 days, during which time all kinds of facilities are made available to the artists,[18] who have to produce in return, some commonly agreed upon number of works. This type of venture may have remote referential potential to evoke the modernist notion of a "camp" as an alternative or utopic space.[19] On the other hand, it also can evoke the modern nation state's attempt to convert the world itself into a camp through various apparatuses of surveillance and control.[20] These two seemingly distinct conceptualizations of camp are evoked here to suggest that the new avatar of "liberal camping" in the field of art embodies phantoms of both. On the one hand, this artists' camp is designed as a temporary utopian space, as well as a space that quarantines a group of artists (through consent) in an obligatory relationship with the organizer. The camp as a modernist alternative, on the other hand, was imagined as a coming together of a possible future community.[21] The idea of sharing was central to this coming together. It was a voluntary act of togetherness, resistance and imagining. The new "camp economy" remotely claims some antecedents to this past but, in effect, functions as a mechanism that erases such possibilities by commercializing the acts of communication, and thereby future communities.

The Exhibitionary Order

In this exploration of modes of artistic production, dissemination and consumption in Baroda, it is crucial to examine, even cursorily, the nature of exhibitions which took place in the city, particularly during the period of economic liberalization. Numerous art shows were organized in all of the newly emerged private art galleries in the city; most of them in the form of loosely framed group exhibitions primarily catering to the corresponding newly emerged, upwardly-mobile, urban middle class. This was also the time that saw new galleries in the metropolitan centres making inroads into the otherwise conventional economy of artistic production in Baroda by supporting large-scale artistic projects by already established artists in order to meet the large demand for Indian art in the global market. The unprecedented capital inflow in general also paved the way for the spectacularization of art and artistic production. In fact, this spectacularization has its correspondence with trends in the global art field.[22]

The spectacularization of art and artistic practices can be understood as an instance of a phantasmagoria[23] of progress wherein market and commodity value are presented as mythic powers capable of producing out of themselves a future world of harmony and abundance. As Susan Buck-Morss has noted, "Everything desirable could be transformed into commodities, as fetishes-on-display that held the crowd enthralled even when personal possession was far beyond their reach. Indeed, an unattainably high price tag only enhanced a commodity's symbolic value. Moreover, when newness became a fetish, history itself became a manifestation of the commodity form."[24] This phantasmagoria has in part been produced through artists undertaking monumental projects within "conventional" practices like painting, sculpture and printmaking, as well as in the name of new practices such as "installation art". But in terms of exhibitionary practices, the experiential dimension of this phantasmagoria is largely produced through the abundance of loosely organized group exhibitions (mostly comprising "emerging" artists) at the FFA Exhibition Hall and at other private galleries in the city.[25]

Interestingly, there have hardly been any curatorial ventures of national or international standing that took place during this period in Baroda.[26] The argument here is not that all curatorial ventures inherently have counter-discourses on spectacularization or fetishization of art works. However, this glaring absence in Baroda of critically acclaimed curated exhibitions, solo exhibitions or retrospective exhibitions of artists from the city, an absence which persisted in spite of the emergence of at least a few equipped galleries, is indicative of some structural inadequacies of the field. This failure to inculcate a culture of critical exhibitionary practices, and thereby a new viewing culture, also contributed to the manner in which the local and the particular remained peripheral to artistic imagination. The argument here is not that this phenomenon is peculiar to Baroda as a provenance, but that such attitudes are more than symptomatic of the ways in which artistic and exhibitionary practices developed in modern India. The irony is that Baroda as a city has had a very high concentration of artists of different age groups and stature; however, there have hardly been any substantive artistic or intellectual "communitas".[27]

We may be able to attribute several reasons for the lack of curatorial initiatives in the context of Baroda. First of all, as mentioned before, Baroda had emerged mostly as an artistic production centre and most of the art works produced here directly catered either to the network of collectors (very often without any form of exhibition) or to exhibitions in metropolitan centres such as Mumbai or Delhi. Second, and concurrent with the first, despite many art galleries that cropped up during the market boom, there were hardly any concerted efforts in the city to develop a new exhibitionary culture based on critical curatorial practices. In that sense, the near absence of any major curatorial intervention from/within Baroda, or any influential curator from the city per se, has its roots in the way in which the historical trajectory of artistic practices and production have been configured within this provenance.

I would further argue that the historical predicament of educational institutional apparatuses and their largely stagnant pedagogic vision has also played a role. At the same time, one may also note that the early millennium witnessed the emergence of fresh areas and methodologies of research in the context of art history and criticism,[28] which included a renewed interest in studies of popular cultures and questions of minorities and marginalities. However, these newer interests in the popular and the public sphere were unable to translate institutionally into developing substantial studies which may have explored the role of critical curatorial discourses in the dissemination of newer ideas regarding art and culture at large. Such developments would undoubtedly have altered the trajectory of exhibitionary practices within Baroda, thereby redefining the nature and role of artistic engagements within the cultural milieu of the city.[29]

Postscript

The attack on a student and some art works (and on FFA as such) in 2007 by majoritarian forces, who alleged that his examination works hurt religious sentiments, is an obvious exemplifier of the way in which the city is communally polarized and culturally intolerant.

12
Chandramohan's work being removed, FFA, May 9, 2007. Photograph: Atreyee Gupta.

At the same time, it signals the growing divide between artistic practices, exhibitionary orders and the "public" at large – a form of insularism cultivated by modernist art practice which needs to be accounted for here. The subsequent incidents leading to the suspension of the then in-charge Dean, followed by artists' and students' agitations, also stand as an evidence of the alienated existence of the Faculty within the cityscape of Baroda. This month-long agitation, mostly led by students of FFA, demonstrated the fragile nature of the artistic community (or lack of a "real-community") within Baroda. At the same time, the way in which the students organized their agitation – largely through innovative visual aids and performative acts – can be understood as one of the few collective attempts to rethink the role of art and exhibitionary orders in the context of art and its relationship with the immediate communities and cultures. In this context, the artist Vivan Sundaram organized the protesting artists and students to collectively transform one of the large studio spaces in the Department of Painting at FFA entirely (from floor to wall) into a captivating act of folding and unfolding of "event-art".[30] The unfolding of this event in a certain sense is imagined as an encounter aimed at unsettling the boundaries between art and non-art, originality and hybridity, the auratic and the blasphemous, viewer and maker, mark-making and erasure, creation and exhibition, spectator and participant; and most importantly (and specific to this context), art and activism. It would be imperative to institutionally and collectively address some of these pertinent issues (that have merely been signposted by this essay) with a greater sense of urgency, intensity and political will. And the argument is that only by the results of such initiatives (however minuscule they may be) can we determine the future of this provenance and its inherited virtues of cosmopolitanism.

13
Creative protests with banners at the FFA, June 26, 2007. Photograph: B.V. Suresh.

14
Forty-hour non-stop drawing workshop organized by Vivan Sundaram with students, artists and faculty members, Department of Painting, FFA, August 13–15, 2007. Photograph: Indrapramit Roy.

Notes

1   Gulammohammed Sheikh, ed., *Contemporary Art in Baroda*, New Delhi: Tulika, 1997.

2   Walter Benjamin, *Moscow Diary*, edited by Gary Smith, Cambridge, Mass.: Harvard University Press, 1986, p. 25.

3   In a Benjaminian sense, the flaneur provides philosophical insight into the nature of modern subjectivity by placing it within specific historical existence. In the flaneur, concretely, we recognize our own consumerist mode of being-in-the-world. The flaneur thus becomes extinct only by exploding into a myriad of forms, the phenomenological characteristics of which, no matter how new they may appear, continue to bear his traces, as Ur-form. This is the "truth" of the flaneur, more visible in his afterlife than in his flourishing. For a detailed discussion on this conception of the flaneur, see Susan Buck-Morss, "The Flâneur, the Sandwichman and the Whore: The Politics of Loitering", *New German Critique,* No. 39, Second Special Issue on Walter Benjamin, Autumn 1986, pp. 99–140.

4   A Vadodara Municipal Corporation bulldozer razed the 300-year-old dargah of Rashiduddin Chishti near Champaner Gate on May 1, 2006. The violence that erupted resulted in the death of six people; 42 were injured, including 16 in police firing. This also led to the imposition of five days' curfew, not to mention further polarization of the population.

5   Sankarshan Thakur, "The Secular Lies of Baroda", *Tehelka* Weekly, May 20, 2006.

6   Thakur provides a graphic historical account of major incidents of communal violence that have taken place in the city over the years. He writes, "It is more a gash cleaved in the minds of its people. 1969. 1971. 1978. 1982. 1983. 1987. 1991. 1992. 1993. 1995. 1998. 2000. 2002. 2002 again and again. 2005. April 2006 .... The tear has been ripped too oft, too savagely for sutures to work."

7   The five-day long exhibition organized by Citizens' Confluence was held from October 2 to 6, 2002 in the Exhibition Hall of the FFA, and saw the participation of around 150 artists from across the country to raise funds for victims of the 2002 violence.

8   Sheikh's works have had a longstanding engagement with questions of the everyday, the familiar and the local in the larger context of communal polarization and stratification of the city and society at large. For instance, *City for Sale* (1981–84) has references to the history of communal riots in Baroda. His series of works such as *Walled City*, *Mappamundi* and *Kaavad*, among many others, also deal with these questions in substantive ways.

9   B.V. Suresh's consistent engagement with multiple aspects of majoritarian politics and culture culminated in a solo exhibition of works titled *Facilitating the Beast*, exhibited at Vadehra Art Gallery, New Delhi in October 2006. Interestingly, this exhibition was not displayed in Baroda.

10 As part of the Gujarat carnage of 2002, on March 1, an extremely violent mob (around 500 in number) attacked the small Muslim-owned Best Bakery on the outskirts of Baroda, and killed 14 people in a 16-hour-long brutality that began around 6 pm and lasted until 10 am the next day.

11 This decade-long project of Vasudha Thozhur's, for which she collaborated with Himmat, an NGO working with marginalized communities in Ahmedabad, culminated in an exhibition in July 2013 titled *Beyond Pain: An Afterlife*, displayed simultaneously at Sakshi Gallery and Project 88, Mumbai. It is important to mention here that this exhibition was conceptualized as a collaborative project where, alongside her works, Thozhur exhibited the works of six young girls who were survivors of the carnage at Naroda Patiya (a neighbourhood in Ahmedabad).

12 The only official public outreach programme was the biennial Fine Arts Fair. The other attraction for the public has been the annual programme of Garba (dance) conducted during the Navaratri festival within the FFA premises, even though participation in the dance is restricted to FFA members and its alumni. The annual display/examination of students' works, which occasioned in 2007 the attack on the FFA by majoritarian forces, has been another, but unofficial event.

13 For instance, Geeta Kapur observes that this process of liberalization and market economy had produced "an enormous, two-hundred-million strong Indian middle class .... [T]his is the

upwardly mobile middle class that is, for the first time, testing its identity vis-a-vis the world. In addition to the middle class, the globalizing Indian bourgeoisie and the NRIs (non-resident Indians) have come into the picture and now constitute the largest section (ninety per cent) of the international buyers." See Geeta Kapur, "What's New in Indian Art: Canons, Commodification, Artists on the Edge", in Pratapaditya Pal, ed., *2000: Reflections on the Arts of India*, Bombay: Marg Publications, 2000.

14 Some examples of art galleries that emerged around this time include Sarjan Art Gallery (earlier a hobby centre), Kaleidoscope Gallery, ABS Gallery and Art Core. One of the earliest initiatives in fact was Nazar Art Gallery (1996–2003), which organized some small but significant exhibitions in the city.

15 Founded by Nandini and Amitabh Gandhi in 1997, ART Underground organized some significant workshops and exhibitions such as the 2001 *New Media Art Workshop* that saw the participation of 20 eminent contemporary artists. Despite the closure of the gallery premises, the promoters continue their effort in supporting new media art practices.

16 The specificity of this "gift-giving" process varies from studio to studio, but the nature of it in all instances is completely determined by the patron. Among the works produced by artists during their residence, conventionally at least one work by each of them is "gifted" in a period of six months (if a 3 x 3 foot canvas, then two works; if a 5 x 6 foot canvas, then one work), or three works in a period of one year, all selected by the patron.

17 Perhaps a cooperative in the true sense of the word, Chhaap was set up in 1999 and is promoted by three Baroda-based printmakers and artists, Gulammohammed Sheikh, Vijay Bagodi and Kavita Shah.

18 This camp "package" often involves an all-expenses-paid trip including sightseeing, museum visits and, very often, provision of raw material for making art works according to the needs of the artists. Artists are also paid an honorarium for participation in the camps. Needless to say, this model of the camp has helped many upcoming artists to sustain themselves in the very competitive and unpredictable climate of the art market.

19 See Susan Sontag, "Notes on 'Camp'", in *Against Interpretation and Other Essays*, UK: Penguin, 2013.

20 See Giorgio Agamben, *Homo Sacer: Sovereign Power and Bare Life*, translated by Daniel Heller-Roazen, Stanford: Stanford University Press, 1998, pp. 174–75, 181. According to Agamben, "The birth of the camp in our time appears as an event which decisively signals the political space of modernity itself." He further identifies the camp as "the fundamental biopolitical paradigm of the West".

21 In the context of modern art practices in India, the two artists' camps organized by the Indian Radical Painters & Sculptors' Association in the 1980s can be considered as one such ideal form of articulation similar to the concepts that Sontag refers to.

22 For instance, "new age" galleries like Bodhi Art supported large-scale artistic projects of some Baroda-based artists, which were mostly exhibited outside Baroda. Bodhi Art also brought to Baroda in 2007 one of the most "spectacular" exhibitions – *Throne of Frost*, by Anju Dodiya, held at the Durbar Hall of the Lakshmi Vilas Palace. *Shri Khakhar Prasanna* by Atul Dodiya, held at the Exhibition Hall of FFA in 2005, is another example of bringing portions of large exhibitions into the city as part of a tribute to its legacy. Yet another instance of a large-scale exhibition visiting Baroda is *LaVA* (Laboratory of Visual Arts, a travelling installation project) by Bose Krishnamachari in 2006, at the ABS Gallery.

23 Marx has used the term phantasmagoria to refer to the deceptive appearances of commodities as "fetishes" in the marketplace. But I use this term more in a Benjaminian sense in order to unearth the buried markers that expose this "progress". Unlike Marx, for Benjamin whose point of departure was a philosophy of historical experience rather than an economic analysis of capital, the key to understanding phantasmagoria was not so much the commodity-in-the-market as the commodity-on-display, where exchange value no less than use value lost practical meaning, and purely representational value came to the fore.

24 Susan Buck-Morss, *Dialectics of Seeing: Walter Benjamin and the Arcades Project*, Cambridge, Mass.: MIT Press, 1991, pp. 81–82.

25 In fact, the FFA Exhibition Hall was over-booked during this period. Galleries like Sarjan held regular shows with hardly any interval. ABS Gallery too held innumerable group exhibitions at that time. A regular show of ABS Gallery such as the *Feb Show* perhaps best illustrates the loosely organized nature of these forms of exhibitionary practices.

26 So also, in this context, it is important to mention that there were hardly any solo exhibitions of works by senior and well-established artists in the city. Most of their exhibitions were held either in metropolises like Mumbai and Delhi or in art galleries and museums abroad. This was also the time when the idea of the mega-show attained wide currency. However, some of these artists organized peer-previews of their shows/works (or a part of them) in Baroda, either in the spaces of their own studios/homes, or at the FFA Exhibition Hall or some private studio space for an invited audience.

27 Victor Turner has used this concept to study rituals and defines *communitas* as an unstructured but common and equal state that community members share by experiencing liminality. See Victor Turner, *Dramas, Fields, and Metaphors: Symbolic Action in Human Society*, Ithaca, NY: Cornell University Press, 1975. However, my usage of the term has no direct reference to the concept coined by Turner. Communitas is used here to evoke the transgressive potential of a community.

28 The Department of Art History and Aesthetics, FFA, under the headship of Professor Shivaji K. Panikkar had undertaken a revision of the pedagogic intent of the discipline which culminated in the formation of what is now known as New Art History. For a detailed understanding, see Shivaji K. Panikkar, Parul Dave Mukherjee and Deeptha Achar, eds., *Towards a New Art History: Studies in Indian Art*, New Delhi: D.K. Printworld, 2003.

29 In fact, there were preliminary attempts in the Department of Art History and Aesthetics, FFA, towards developing a curriculum for critical curatorial practice/studies with the assistance of the India Foundation for the Arts from 2005 to 2007, either through initiating a Master's programme in Curatorial Practice, or through the introduction of some courses on critical curatorial studies. However, the unprecedented events of May 2007 sabotaged these and many other possibilities.

30 This 40-hour non-stop drawing workshop held from August 13–15, 2007, comprised various acts of art – for example, artists, students and others making continuous improvisations on a drawing, to the extent that each making involved some form of unmaking; towards the end, in a symbolic gesture, all the "works" were removed from the space and ritualistically burned to ashes amidst sloganeering and chanting by the participants.

Art in Baroda: Provincial Location, Cosmopolitan Aspiration

Chaitanya Sambrani

I am a citizen of the world.
> – Diogenes[1]

To us all towns are one, all men our kin.
> – Kaniyan Poongundranar[2]

At a prominent street corner in the Fatehgunj[3] district of the modern city of Baroda, and opposite the Centenary Methodist Church (built 1880), stands Cafe Cosmopolitan,[4] long a haunt of lovers of biryani, fried fish, chicken and eggs in a city lately dominated by strident adherents of vegetarianism founded on neo-Hindu ideology. Since this essay was first drafted, "Cosmo" has shut its doors for good, perhaps a reflection of declining patronage. Further down University Road (Professor Chandravadan Mehta Marg) from Cosmo is a gaslamp-lit assemblage of handcart-eateries (locally known as laaris) specializing in a variety of cuisines, including vegetarian and vegan-friendly versions of regional Indian, as well as "Chinese", "Thai" and "Italian" food, interspersed with those offering the pleasures of spicy omelettes.

Within a kilometre of each other these formal and informal enterprises are geared to the appreciation and consumption of *difference* in a remarkably self-conscious manner. The sign on Cosmo declares it as "non-veg." with the red dot logo used to label food-products as such (sometimes a brown dot is used for this purpose). A green dot placed at the side indicates that "vegetarian" dishes are also on the menu. Most of the laaris too distinguish themselves with red (and/or) green dot logos to declare their affiliations. This clear display of differentiation guides consumers to their preferred destination. The boards indicating the laariwalas' culinary specializations further guide consumer choice: Chinese or Thai, Indian or Italian, vegetarian or otherwise.

Arguably, this desire to appreciate (and consume) difference is a signifier of the claim that the cosmopolitan mind makes upon the world. At the very least, such appreciation allows for a "universalist" levelling: despite our differences, urban citizens in a globalized world are able to abide by essentially the same systems of production, dissemination and consumption when it comes to aesthetic (or gastronomic) enjoyment. Herein is also signalled an oft-repeated critique of the cosmopolitan imagination: that it subjects cultural (and other) differences to a false levelling of the playing field in the name of aspirational belonging. This essay seeks to consider the problematic of provincial location and cosmopolitan aspiration in the context of the visual art culture of modern Baroda, and the "being and belonging"[5] that are implicit in both. Remaining rooted in a provincial sense of being while aspiring to belong in a cosmopolis of the imagination is perhaps the central point of the dialectic pertinent to Baroda, one case among other locations across several national contexts. The "Baroda" of this essay is inevitably a network rather than a site, insofar as contestations and affiliations with Bombay, Delhi, Santiniketan as well as places much further afield are integral to the Baroda story.[6]

Location and Aspiration

The aspiration to partake of a cosmopolitan lifestyle while being securely located in a provincial culture is a highlight of popular culture in Baroda. Such is also the case in the academy-trained visual arts. This aspiration is not without attendant complications. As Gerard Delanty has suggested, "cosmopolitanism represents the immanent possibilities within modernity and which has often been contained within nationalism as an unrealized potential."[7] I am sure that most of the consumers of "world cuisine" on the streets of Fatehgunj and adjacent Pratapgunj[8] do not consciously think of themselves as being particularly cosmopolitan. In fact, I suspect many of them hold deeply parochial and provincial attitudes as evidenced in the high level of support among the Gujarati middle class for Hindu nationalist politics.[9] Nevertheless, the aspiration towards cosmopolitanism, even if at the level of consumption, tells a significant story. "Cosmopolitanist" thought has become an alternative to Enlightenment ideas of "political life based on reason".[10] The academic discourse on visual art in Baroda (as elsewhere in India and other postcolonial nations) has followed suit in its implicit critique of singular notions of national culture. Rather than homogeneity within the construct of a unitary national imagination, this discourse privileges a claim to diversity and difference. Belonging is articulated within the margins of nationhood and in the liminal zones of the regional, the national and the international.

1
"Cosmopolitan non-veg. restaurant", Fatehgunj, 2014. Photograph accessed from the Internet.

2
Centenary Methodist Church, Fatehgunj, built 1880.

3
Cafe Cosmopolitan, now shut down, 2015.

4
Laari-walas (handcart food-vendors) at Prof.
Chandravadan Mehta Marg/University
Road, 2014.

5
Facade of the Painting Department, FFA with
cement relief mural by K.G. Subramanyan.
On the left is artist Jalendu Dave.

6
Returning Home after Long Absence, by
Gulammohammed Sheikh, 1969–73.
Oil on canvas; 122 x 122 cm. Collection:
Ram and Bharati Sharma, New Delhi.
Photograph courtesy the artist.

Diogenes was a resident of the Greek *polis* (city-state) of Sinope when he claimed world-
citizenship. This was long before it was possible to speak of a Greek nation-state. Implicit
in his announcement was a critique of the limitations posed by secure belonging within
the remit of the city-state. Commenting on Diogenes, Nussbaum has suggested, "He
meant by this, it appears, that he refused to be defined by his local origins and local group
memberships, so central to the self-image of a conventional Greek male."[11] This refusal to
conform to narrow definitions of belonging continues to resonate in contemporary culture,
especially in the context of increasing tensions around migration, asylum and contested
borders in many parts of the world. Nussbaum has also made the crucial distinction between
a local community (that of birth) and an aspirational community (that of argument, or
of intellectual projection) in relation to cosmopolitan belonging.[12] And it is precisely this
question of belonging in both of these communities that is central to the Baroda experience
of provincial location and cosmopolitan aspiration.

Gulammohammed Sheikh (b. 1937), an early alumnus of the Faculty of Fine Arts has said
of his student years, "we always looked at our contemporaries, our peers and our elders … it
was a sense of history that [we] always tried to connect [to] … [to] see how others have done
[things] in the past …."[13] It was important for this generation of artists to pay attention to the
example of teachers such as K.G. Subramanyan (b. 1924) and N.S. Bendre (1910–92) who

7
Janata Watch Repairing, by Bhupen
Khakhar, 1972. Oil on canvas; 93.5 x
93.5 cm. Collection of Vivan Sundaram.
Courtesy of Gallery Chemould Archive.

manifested in their work the commingling of influences from high and low art, indigenous
and foreign tendencies. This was especially marked in Subramanyan's discourse geared towards
the creation of what he famously called a "living tradition".[14] The cosmopolitan aspiration
in Baroda has always been accompanied – and complicated – by an abiding desire for local
belonging and community. This complication is inevitable in a postcolonial and polycultural,
polyglot, multi-ethnic context such as that of India, where identities are often palimpsests,
and the preservation of local forms of difference remains an important objective alongside
the desire to participate in and partake of the national construct as well as the wider world.

Importantly for Sheikh and a number of his colleagues including Bhupen Khakhar (1934–
2003), it was essential to find this sense of history and belonging both in the local, birth
community, and in the aspirational community of an artistic and art-historical cosmopolis.
Sheikh and Khakhar construed this duality differently. Sheikh privileged an erudite embrace
of Asian and European art history, and a sense of polyform belonging: "The world as it came
to me … [was] almost invariably manifold …. The multiplicity and simultaneity of these
worlds filled me with a sense of being part of them all."[15] Khakhar chose the somewhat
more wilful and mischievous path of embracing the popular and the kitsch as seen in his
declarations such as, "A bouquet of plastic flowers is an eternal joy to the eyes."[16] Khakhar's
engagement with small-town characters and situations marked a pointedly critical and yet

sympathetically humorous approach to the ephemeral margins of modern society as well as the aspirational cosmopolitanism of the emergent middle class in mofussil India.

There are two ways of understanding the allure of the cosmopolitan: one from the locus of staking territory and the right to belong, the other from that of extending generous hospitality. These two ways are foreshadowed in the two epigraphs at the beginning of this essay: Diogenes makes a *claim* to world citizenship, whereas Poongundranar's verse implies a sense of *generosity* in proffering universal kinship, declaring familiarity with all places and filial ties with all people. This tenor of generosity is also highlighted in the much-quoted Sanskrit shloka:

Ayam bandhurayam neti ganana laghuchetasam
Udaracharitanam tu vasudhaiva kutumbakam

Only small men discriminate saying: one is a relative; the other is a stranger.
For those who live magnanimously the entire world constitutes but a family.

– *Mahōpaniśad*, Ch. 6, V. 72[17]

There are deep histories of hospitable cosmopolitanism within the Indian tradition as iterated in advaita (non-dualist) philosophy, and in the poetry of Bhakti and Sufi saint-poets of the Indian subcontinent.[18] Witness for instance, the poet Kabir (c. 1440–1518) declaring an oceanic commingling of the self with others:

In every direction I see only a collection and carnival of me. I am in everybody and everybody is in me.[19]

It would seem to be in the same spirit that Sheikh speaks:

Anything that you love very deeply, [becomes] part of your own consciousness … part of your being …. Your being harbours a space … to allow [that which is loved] to inhabit.[20]

Claiming versus Belonging

The position of the claimant is important in postcolonial terms, as an aspect of wagering on an empowered subjectivity untrammelled by anxieties of influence. The postcolonial subject makes a claim, carving out a position in modernity that is self-consciously different from the normative narrative of the Euro-American modern.[21] Alongside the trading ports of peninsular India which maintained contacts with eastern Africa, western Asia, Europe and Southeast Asia, its land borders with Central and West Asia (and consequently Europe), and with Tibet and China have been formative in the development of Indian culture and art. Deep histories of contact between indigenous and foreign civilizations are central to the variegated character of Indian culture. The experience of European colonization adds to and further complicates this mixed inheritance. It is not surprising, therefore, that the assertion of a multiple inheritance and cosmopolitan belonging emerges as a distinctive feature of postcolonial thought in contemporary India. Likewise, the uneven and often violent contact with modernity has resulted in the emergence of several hybrid forms of culture that both Khakhar and Sheikh remained attentive to.

There are three precedents that I would like to address here, as a way of situating the relevance of cosmopolitan thought in modern Indian art, especially in the Baroda context. The first comes from W.E. Gladstone Solomon, who as Principal of Bombay's Sir J.J. School of Art made a point of separating the sphere of art education from that of anti-colonial political ferment. Founded in 1857, nearly a century before the FFA in Baroda, the J.J. School stood alongside Kala Bhavan and Santiniketan as one of the two possible origin-models for the FFA. The fact that several of the early teachers at Baroda had connections with one or other of these schools meant a transfer of impulses from Bombay or Bengal, modified to suit the new curriculum. Solomon's description of the audience at an award-giving ceremony held on the J.J. School grounds on February 14, 1922 as part of the Prince of Wales' visit is revealing:

> The costumes of the Europeans contrasted with the Indian dresses, and broken by a large sprinkling of white "Gandhi" caps showed emblematically the catholicity of that appeal which the School of Art ought to make to its public. For the School's compound is neutral ground where rival factions fraternally mix, where Cosmopolitan hearts beat in unison to the gentle but irresistible music of Saraswati's Vina which can still the pulsations of Politics, or the frettings of Commerce, as sweetly as did the harp of Orpheus the fierce prowlers of the Dorian Forests.[22]

Art for Solomon evidently carried universal appeal, something the indigenist ideology of Santiniketan resisted, even though the pan-Asian experiment at Santiniketan fusing elements of Indian, Chinese, Japanese and European influences did constitute a sort of cosmopolitanism.[23] In Solomon's account, the J.J. School of Art figured as a temple where the Hindu goddess of knowledge reigned supreme over base passions such as politics and economics, with her gentle but forceful presence evacuating the campus of any contentious political issues. Nationalists wearing caps of hand-spun, hand-woven khadi mixed in this temple with others sporting European costume, all in tune with the calling of "Cosmopolitan hearts" whether inspired by Minerva or by Saraswati. Solomon's attitude mirrored that of other British Orientalists, as in the case of the India Society (established 1907). And yet, the avowedly apolitical pursuit of Orientalist scholarship was a manifestly political exercise, even as it was implicated in the production of imperial knowledge, and colonial forms of culture. Coupled with what Bernard Cohn has called the modalities of historiography, of observation/travel, of survey, enumeration, museumization and surveillance, this epistemological project forms one of the roots of what we understand as modern Indian cultural identity, the other root ensuing from nationalist and presumably anti-Orientalist assertions of either materialist or idealist persuasion.[24] That the idealist argument for national emancipation feeds into a kind of auto-Orientalism is a moot point, though it is certainly borne out in modernist critiques of the Bengal School.

My second historical precedent comes from a close friend (as well as occasional antagonist) of artists from "the Baroda School", J. Swaminathan (1928–94). In his argumentative manifesto for the 1963 exhibition of Group 1890, Swaminathan declared (all in lower case),

> from its early beginnings in the vulgar naturalism of raja raviverma [sic] and the pastoral idealism of the bengal school, down through hybrid mannerisms resulting from the imposition of concepts evolved by successive art movements in modern european art on classical, miniature and folk style to the flight into "abstraction" in the name of cosmopolitanism, tortured alternately by memories of a glorious past born out of a sense of futility in the face of a dynamic present and the urge to catch up with the times so as to merit recognition, modern indian art has by and large been inhibited by the self-defeating purposiveness of its attempts at establishing identity.

8

Mephistopheles ... Otherwise, the Quaquaversal Prolix, The Doctrine of the Forest. Cuckoonebulopolis, by Surendran Nair, 2003. Oil on canvas; 210 x 120 cm. Photograph: Krause & Johansen.

Cosmopolitanism for Swaminathan was in this instance aligned with an escape into vacuous internationalism. His later work as artist, curator and ideologue notably developed a vision of contemporaneity that was not restricted to the academy-trained urban artist in India, but sought to establish a parallel position in modernity for the adivasi (indigenous tribal) artist. Swaminathan's manifesto for the inaugural (and only) exhibition of Group 1890 has since been historicized as a significant critique of national modernism in Indian art, be it in the nature of romantic idealization, expressionist anguish or abstract universalism.

The third precedent for this essay is particular to the institutional context of Baroda. It again serves to reiterate a sense of Baroda being network rather than site. Over several issues in 1972–73, *Vrishchik* (Scorpio; a "little journal" co-edited by Sheikh and Khakhar) carried a serialized essay by Delhi-based critic and curator Geeta Kapur (b. 1943).[25] "In Quest of Identity: Art and Indigenism in postcolonial culture with special reference to contemporary Indian painting" was Kapur's MA thesis submitted to the Royal College of Art, London, completed under the guidance of Peter de Francia. For Kapur and her generation, a move away from universalist modernism and an investigation of "what nationality and regionality meant" was the most pressing concern of the 1970s.

In addition to presenting a critique of Western modernism, and surveying the search for Indian-ness in early-20th-century art, Kapur analysed the drive towards internationalism in Indian art before coming to the question of indigenism during the 1960s. Calling for a renewed analysis of the conditions and historical relationships of modern art in India, she presented a polemical argument against nostalgic insularity as well as blind cosmopolitanism, and in favour of a nuanced indigenism, declaring: "Cultural indigenism attempts to dig up the soil and make it fertile again."[26] Kapur issued a caution against a pseudo-renaissance or revival. For her, indigenism would have to transcend stylistic change; it could only be radical if it broke through "the parasitical nostalgia that clings to Indian culture … as well as … complacent and imitative cosmopolitanism".[27] For

9
The Arrival of Vasco da Gama (after an 1898 painting by Jose Veloso Salgado), by Pushpamala N., 2014. Photo performance: archival inkjet print on canvas, 152 x 229 cm with gold frame, installed with painted backdrops, props, blackboard, wooden desk, globe, texts and process photographs. Photograph courtesy the artist and Nature Morte, New Delhi.

Kapur, cosmopolitanism in this instance was aligned with an internationalist language of abstraction, which she was later to contrast against a propensity to figuration and synthesis through narrative that she argued was inalienably native to the Indian tradition.[28]

Absolute Belonging and the Limits of Cosmopolitan Imagination

Making a case for "cities of refuge" in the European context, Jacques Derrida asked whether it was possible to make "a legitimate distinction between the two forms of the metropolis – the City and the State."[29] Seeking to reinscribe them into contemporary discourse and policy, Derrida called for "an original concept of hospitality" that incorporated both the duty of hospitality and the right to hospitality.[30] In the Indian context, metropolitan ambitions are being prominently articulated by several cities and by the nation-state, although the idea of hospitable cosmopolitanism seems conspicuously absent in putting these aspirations into practice. Arguably, the Baroda of this essay – network rather than site – has been a "city of refuge", at least in terms of the art scene. Several generations of artists from Kerala, Maharashtra, Bengal, Tamil Nadu, Assam, Karnataka and elsewhere have come to learn and settle in Baroda, even though the development of fundamentalist intolerance in recent decades has undermined this position. Derrida was only referring to a geopolitical duty of extending hospitality in the context of the right to asylum and a "*renewal* of international law". The history of the FFA in Baroda bears witness to the efforts of students and artists who have sought to marry lives that are, as Nussbaum states, based "less on reason and more on communal solidarity, less on principle and more on affiliation, less on optimism for progress than on a sober acknowledgement of human finitude".[31] Like the handcart-eateries of my introduction, there are persistent claims on the cosmopolitan imagination in the work of contemporary Indian artists. For instance, looking at recent work by Pushpamala N., Anita Dube, Surendran Nair and Nataraj Sharma (all born in the mid-1950s and students at the FFA during the 1980s), it becomes evident that the dialectic between local belonging and

10
Urban Animal (Horse), by Nataraj Sharma, 2012. Oil on canvas; 244 x 366 cm (two panels). In the background is the gate of Kamatibaug/Sayajibaug, at the Kalaghoda circle. Photograph courtesy the artist.

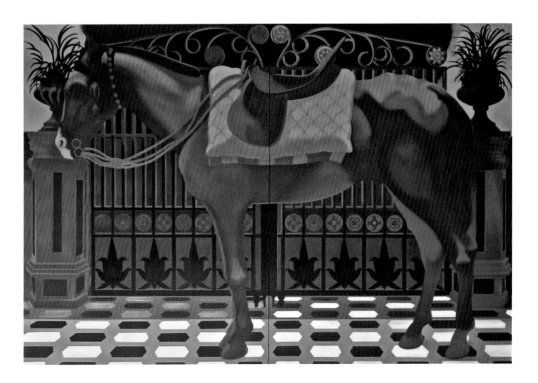

cosmopolitan aspiration continues to be a locus of exploration. For artists in contemporary India, it has been important to claim absolute belonging in modernity. Whereas the European modern has been primarily defined by the historical discourse of the Enlightenment and its claim on the universal, many artists in/from Baroda have persisted in pursuing the cosmopolitan to test the limits of belonging in a political environment that manifestly seeks to regulate and enforce forms of conformity and assimilation.

Notes

1   Although commonly attributed to Diogenes of Sinope (Greek Cynic philosopher, c. 412–373 BCE), the statement is of Socratic origin, according to Nikos Papastergiadis. See his *Cosmopolitanism and Culture*, Cambridge: Polity Press, 2012, p. 81.

2   A Tamil Sangam poet whose dates are uncertain (between 3rd century BCE and 4th century CE). The quotation is the first line of Poongundranar's poem "*Yaadhum Oore Yaavarum Kelir*" which is verse 192 in the Sangam compendium *Purananuru* (translated by the Christian missionary and scholar G.U. Pope [1820–1908] in 1906). Pope's translation can be found in *Tamil Heroic Poems*, Madras: South India Shaiva Siddhanta Works Publishing Company, 1973, as well as on a number of sites on the Internet.

3   Named after Fatehsingh Rao Gaekwad (1930–88), titular Maharaja of Baroda, 1951–71.

4   Cafe Cosmopolitan was established in 1968, and was originally owned by a Keralite Muslim by the name of Abdul Hamid Chakra. My thanks to Baroda artist Anandajit Ray, who supplied the name of Chakra as the original owner, in a phone conversation, April 28, 2014.

5   Papastergiadis, 2012.

6   As opposed to colonial-era art schools in Bombay (Mumbai), Madras (Chennai), Calcutta (Kolkata) and Santiniketan, the FFA in Baroda was established after Independence, and drew its early teachers from the older schools. These individuals brought their different convictions and experiences to bear in formulating the directions that the new school was to pursue. The regular presence of visiting artists from within India and overseas further added to a sense of network rather than site.

7   Gerard Delanty, *The Cosmopolitan Imagination: The Renewal of Critical Social Theory*, Cambridge: Cambridge University Press, 2009, p. 19.

8   Named after Fatehsingh's father, Pratapsingh (r. 1938–51), the son of Maharaja Sayajirao Gaekwad III (r. 1875–1939). Sayajirao is regarded as the founding father of modern Baroda. Both Fatehgunj and Pratapgunj are "newer" parts of this rapidly expanding city, to the west of the Vishwamitri river, while the old city lies primarily to the east of the river.

9   Current Prime Minister Narendra Modi from the Hindu nationalist Bharatiya Janata Party was elected to Parliament from the Baroda (Vadodara) as well as Banaras (Varanasi) constituencies. He has since resigned his Vadodara seat, retaining Varanasi with its more prominent links to Hindu sacral culture.

10 Martha C. Nussbaum, "Kant and Cosmopolitanism", in Garrett Wallace Brown and David Held, eds., *The Cosmopolitanism Reader*, Cambridge: Polity Press, 2010, p. 27.

11 Ibid., p. 29.

12 Ibid.

13 Gulammohammed Sheikh, interviewed by the author, December 29, 2011.

14 See K.G. Subramanyan, *The Living Tradition: Perspectives on Modern Indian Art*, Calcutta (Kolkata): Seagull Books, 1987.

15 Gulammohammed Sheikh, "Among Several Cultures and Times", in Carla Borden, ed., *Contemporary Indian Tradition*, Washington and London: Smithsonian Institution Press, 1989, p. 108.

16 Bhupen Khakhar, artist's statement, in *Six Who Declined to Show at the Triennale*, exhibition catalogue, New Delhi: Kumar Gallery, 1978.

17 This shloka appears as well in other various Sanskrit texts of didactic import, including the *Hitopadesa* and *Panchatantra*. Dates of composition are varied and continue to be debated.

18 Such traditions are not particular to the subcontinent, and can be found in many different world cultures, with "approximations of cosmopolitan thought" being discernible in ancient works of Egyptian, Phaeacian, Hebrew, Chinese, Ethiopian, Assyrian and Persian cultures. "Editors' Introduction", in Brown and Held, eds., 2010, pp. 3–4.

19 This comes from Kabir's bhajan "*Avadhoota, yuganyugan ham yogi*" (O mystic wanderer, for ages and ages have I been a yogi).

20 Gulammohammed Sheikh, interviewed by the author, December 29, 2011.

21 I refer to Geeta Kapur's formulation "A Stake in Modernity: Brief History of Contemporary Indian Art", in Caroline Turner, ed., *Tradition and Change: Contemporary Art of Asia and the Pacific*, Brisbane: University of Queensland Press, 1993, pp. 27–44. See also John Clark's pioneering study, *Modern Asian Art*, Sydney: Craftsman House, 1998.

22 W.E. Gladstone Solomon, *The Bombay Revival of Indian Art*, Bombay: Sir J.J. School of Art, 1924, p. 76. Solomon's capitalizes both words: cosmopolitan and commerce.

23 There is considerable scholarship on this issue, including: Ratan Parimoo, *The Paintings of the Three Tagores: Abanindranath, Gaganendranath, Rabindranath: Chronology and Comparative Study*, Baroda: Maharaja Sayajirao University Press, 1973; Tapati Guha-Thakurta, *The Making of a New "Indian" Art: Artists, Aesthetics and Nationalism in Bengal, c. 1850–1920,* Cambridge: Cambridge University Press, 1992; R. Siva Kumar, "The Santiniketan Murals: A Brief History", in *The Santiniketan Murals*, Calcutta: Seagull Books, 1995; R. Siva Kumar, *Santiniketan: The Making of a Contextual Modernism*, New Delhi: National Gallery of Modern Art, 1997.

24 Bernard S. Cohn. *Colonialism and Its Forms of Knowledge: The British in India*, Princeton: Princeton University Press, 1996, pp. 5–11.

25 Kapur has remained a regular visitor to Baroda, and was the principal theorist and interlocutor of the "narrative figuration" in painting that Sheikh and Khakhar's generation came to be known for.

26 Geeta Kapur, "In Quest of Identity …", *Vrishchik*, Year 3, Nos. 8–9, June–July 1972.

27 Ibid.

28 Geeta Kapur, "Partisan Views About the Human Figure", catalogue essay, *Place for People*, New Delhi and Mumbai, 1981.

29 Jacques Derrida, "On Cosmopolitanism", in Brown and Held, eds., 2010, p. 413.

30 Ibid., p. 414.

31 Nussbaum, 2010, p. 27.

After 2007:
Towards the Art of Quietness

Deeptha Achar

It is tempting to think of May 9, 2007 as a watershed in the self-imagination of the artist community in Baroda. The day marks the entry of a minor functionary of the Bharatiya Janata Party (BJP) Vadodara Unit into the Faculty of Fine Arts at the Maharaja Sayajirao University. The protest against the alleged obscenity of a student's examination art work triggered a whole series of events: the arrest of the student, a protracted agitation of teachers and students that lasted months, a fact-finding inquiry instituted by the Gujarat Governor, the suspension and eventual resignation of the in-charge Dean of the Faculty.[1] Subsequently, new lines of research that drew from contemporary debates on identity, as well as some frameworks proposed by cultural studies that had opened up at the Department of Art History and Aesthetics, looped back into prior disciplinary orientations.[2] In other words, 2007 seems to mark a moment where the political underpinnings of aesthetic practice took on a public face.

However, it is necessary to locate 2007, momentous as it was, in a longer track in which art practice had perforce to engage with the politics of the aesthetic. As Karin Zitzewitz reminds us, this involves not only works of art but institutional practices that house these works. The "Husain Affair", as she terms it, is certainly a key event in a trajectory that has pit public opinion against art practice.[3] Its similarity with the FFA events would need to be located in the positioning of cultural nationalists, broadly the Hindu Right, vis-a-vis styles of aesthetic representations of the religious read as obscene. In the Husain case, this was exacerbated on account of Husain's Muslim identity. Yet, it might be productive to read FFA in 2007 also in the context of a local trajectory.

I suggest two key moments to situate the 2007 events; one, the broad FFA opposition to the poster campaign organized in 1991 by Gulammohammed Sheikh and like-minded students to uphold secular values, and two, the significant participation of the artist community of Baroda, including the student community of the FFA, in the first peace rallies organized to protest anti-Muslim violence in March 2002. Read together, these events seem to tell a confused tale. On one hand the 1991 events suggest that what appears at first view a liberal apolitical space is not quite so; more, it is a far more politically heterogeneous space than is often assumed. On the other, the students of the FFA emerge as politically oppositional, drawing significantly from the left liberal ethos of the art community generally and of the Faculty more specifically.

Read against this background, the events that have followed 2007 need to be thought across multiple axes.

I attempt in this essay to trace, somewhat schematically, the aftermath of the events of 2007 for the art community in Baroda generally and the student community in particular. What I will not attempt is an overarching survey of art work produced in Baroda since 2007. Instead I track the idea of a "viewing public" in order to read its implications for art practice. I first look at the category of the viewing public as it gets modulated through the 2007 protests; and then discuss some consequences of the 2007 event.

The Question of a Viewing Public

The idea of a viewing public in a sense is embedded in the very process of art production. However, the question of the viewing public is one that has come to preoccupy the art community of Baroda in new ways from 2002 onwards. For example, a considerable number of artists and art students who were involved with making anti-violence posters and banners confronted this question head-on. While devising visual material for dharnas and rallies, and later also when designing posters and pamphlets during the run-up to elections, artists were confronted with questions about visual literacy. Needing to speak to "the people", they found it critical to engage with the viewing public. They were forced to acknowledge the distance of their visual repertoire from the visual range accessible to the public. Thus, they increasingly thought about the gap between the visual universe from which they drew their images and the repertoire of the spectators whom they sought to address.

The question of who sees what can actually be the key question that structures the 2007 moment as well. When the news of the student's arrest broke, the immediate reaction of the art community, in the FFA, in Baroda and elsewhere, was one of outrage, articulated in terms of an attack on the freedom of expression. This argument had already been put forward through the consolidation of the art community's broadly secular position on Husain. Articulated powerfully by SAHMAT, among others, this position invoked the Indian Constitution as a guarantee to the freedom of expression that the artist, as citizen, has a right to enjoy.[4] Such a position, however, becomes hard to maintain when confronted with anti-secular articulations which equally claim constitutional guarantees.

Since at the FFA, the allegations of obscenity and the hurting of sentiments were made in the name of the viewing public, the freedom of expression defence could have but little value. The hurting of sentiment argument also has the tendency of producing the idea of the viewing public in homogeneous terms. However, the heterogeneity of those who view, and the multiplicity of spectatorial locations, is clearly evident in what followed: a display of erotica was assembled by the students of the FFA following the arrest. The display clearly hinged on a perceived gap between the artist community's *visual proficiency* and art-historical expertise, contrasted with the *visual illiteracy* of the common public; artists believed that this gap could be bridged with the "right" education that they could provide.[5] The paternalist structure of such a framework needs to be recognized, as also its location in the idea of the artist as *avant-garde*, which is constituted by the marking of a distance between the artist and society in general.

The exhibition's acknowledgement of a heterogeneous viewing public divided across the line of expertise needs to be set against the fact that the FFA, the arrested student and the

1
Posters on a door in the Graphics Department, as part of creative protests at the FFA, May 12, 2007. Photograph: B.V. Suresh.

suspended Dean received very little support, whether from the larger student community of the University or from the "common" public of Baroda. To explain this away as a simple support for cultural-nationalism or any political party would reduce the significance of a different kind of visual repertoire at play in the public sphere. The discomfort with the art work in question could equally have been generated from its iconography which was disturbingly different from conventional religious imagery: for the most part, especially in urban contexts, Hindu practitioners draw from the provenance of Raja Ravi Varma's gods and goddesses. Anjolie Ela Menon has said "Only since Ravi Varma clothed gods did today's prudery begin taking roots."[6] Further, the self-constructed exclusivity of the FFA, underlined by gestures such as the display of historical erotica, precluded meaningful alliances between the FFA and the public.[7]

However, the events of 2007 also engage another kind of debate on the nature of the viewing public. This debate is located in the manner in which the university is envisaged: what is the nature of the domain that the university inhabits? Funded by the State and imagined as a public institution, it seems to be valid to claim that the university is firmly situated in the public sphere. Yet this claim came to be questioned as the strike wore on. Gradually, the focus moved away from the obscenity of the art work to the jurisdiction of the police and, indeed, the right of the public at large to view the art work at all. At this point FFA students argued that the art work was on display during an examination; therefore, regardless of whether it was obscene or not, it had to be considered as "outside" the purview of the public, particularly at a point when it was being examined. Although the M.S. University Enquiry Committee held that the works were on public display, the fact that the examination jury had not finished the examination process complicated the status of the works – were they open to the public for viewing or not? Girish Karnad states the case powerfully:

> In this case, the self-expression was not made in public but in the private domain. Thus no outsider was affected. If this action of the police becomes an accepted precedent, no one in this country will be safe from invasion of his or her privacy. The student was creating a work as part of his academic course. Only his teacher or examiner or head of department had the right to decide whether the work was acceptable. In any teaching institute, the freedom of the teachers and students to take up for exploration controversial, even unpleasant, topics has to be safeguarded. This is precisely why universities are guaranteed autonomy, and outside organs, like the police, are prohibited entry.[8]

In line with Karnad's argument, the students' position implied that the university is a "special kind of public space", one in which the autonomy of critical thinking and experimentation had to be protected, a public place not quite freely open to the public.

The events of 2007 can thus be seen as engaging with the idea of the viewing public, not only in the students' initial claim that public sentiment cannot encroach upon freedom of expression, but also in their subsequent assertion that the university is a specialized public domain which is marked away from a common public sphere. In the structure of the second claim one can find a certain recognition that there circulate potent public readings of art works that are shaped by visual repertoires and ideological fields that exist outside the informed readings of specialists. Such a recognition would also gesture at the ideological character of disciplinary readings of art works.

2
Students with their posters and banners in front of the FFA office, as part of the creative protests, June 20, 2007. Photograph: B.V. Suresh.

An Inward Turn: Authority and Quietness

The ramifications of the events of 2007 have been many. The intense focus on the idea of a viewing public has wrought significant institutional changes in the sense that there is now considerable attention given to screening of works displayed at the FFA, whether by students at the time of the examination display or by those who hire the FFA Gallery for exhibitions. The general public is no more allowed access to the annual examination display before the jury has evaluated the work. The institutional apparatus that used to exercise nominal control over displays and performances of any kind now wields relatively more

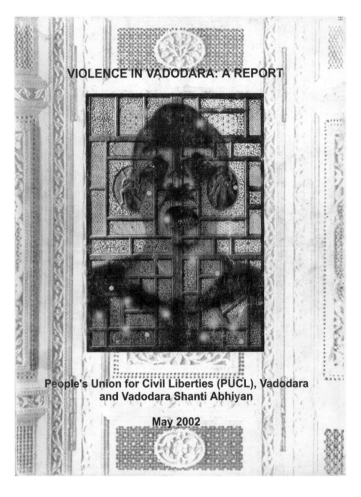

3
Cover of *Violence in Vadodara: A Report*, by PUCL and Vadodara Shanti Abhiyan (Vadodara: Bharti Printers, May 2002). Cover design by Ajay Sharma, alumnus of FFA. Photograph: Rashmimala Devi.

authority. There is today provision for review of work put up at the FFA by a committee drawn substantially from outside.

The 2007 events have also instituted a hyper-vigilant relationship between the local media and political groups with the displays at the FFA. This is evident when we look at protests at the FFA that have led to art works being taken off display. In December 2012, Vishwa Hindu Parishad (VHP) leaders protested against what they termed as the objectionable representations of Shiva and Parvati by the artist Surpal Singh Slathia at the FFA Gallery. Neither Slathia's clarification that he had painted bahurupias (wandering performers) in the garb of Shiva nor his apology for hurting sentiments sufficed, and the exhibition was closed down. The protest led to the Vice Chancellor announcing the constitution of a new committee that comprised the FFA Dean and members, along with two senate members, a dean of another faculty nominated by the Vice Chancellor, two artists nominated by the Syndicate, and two members of society, including a woman. This committee would review all art works put up at the FFA.[9]

The VHP protest came hard at the heels of a local Congress protest in September 2012. Congress workers had likened a work by artist Satyajit Balmik, *Indian Bull Fight*, exhibited at the HUB 5 Group Show at the FFA Exhibition Hall, to that of the cartoonist Aseem Trivedi who had been charged with sedition for his ironic representations of national emblems; it was claimed that Balmik's work was an insult to the Ashoka Chakra. Clarifications issued by the show's organizers were to no avail and the work was taken

4
Report on *Voices against Violence*, news item, *The Indian Express* (Vadodara), October 2, 2002. Photograph: Indrapramit Roy.

5
Banner on the wall outside the FFA, as part of *Voices against Violence*: Artists against Communalism exhibition organized by Vadodara Shanti Abhiyan, Sahaj, and Citizens' Confluence, October 2–6, 2002. Photograph: Indrapramit Roy.

The Indian **EXPRESS**

VADODARA | WEDNESDAY | OCTOBER 2, 2002

Paintings being put up on the walls of the Fine Arts Hall for an exhibition which opens on October 2. *Newsline photo by Bhupendra Rana*

Through art, they raise voice against violence

EXPRESS NEWS SERVICE
VADODARA, OCT 1

'VOICES Against Violence' is a window of vistas to the torn social milieu in present-day society. However, in an endeavour to bridge the crevice of sectarian communalism, 138 city-based artists will try to express their thoughts and responses on the canvases with splashes of colour or through photographs at the five-day exhibition that begins at Fine Arts Faculty from Wednesday.

The exhibition will be organised by Citizens Confluence, an organisation of concerned citizens of Vadodara. "As artists and concerned citizens of the city, we regard it as our duty to help create civic spaces for positive debate to fill in the void in our social structures in danger of being submerged by fundamentalism, and would like to negotiate this process using all the cultural tools at our disposal," say the confluence members.

Artists from all walks of life will exhibit their work, including paintings, drawings, artist's prints, photographs and digital art. The exhibition aims at raising funds for riot victims. The proceeds will be channelised through NGO Vadodara Shanti Abhiyan working for rehabilitation of riot victims in the city.

'Voices of Violence' has taken more than two months to come to reality. It is intended to open a dialogue with audiences and make cultural understanding responsive. Noted artists like Bhupen Khakkar, Dhruva Mistry, Gulam M Sheikh, Nagji Patel, Rekha Rodwittiya, Vivan Sundaram and Jyoti Bhatt will participate in the exhibition. "As artists to help raise funds for a cause like this is the best thing we can do," says Shibu Natesan, another artist.

down.[10] It is significant that, regardless of which political group played the vigilante and for what reason, the FFA has clearly been under continuous public scrutiny.

Post 2007, in spite of being under such intense vigilance, the FFA has been relatively free of public intervention, at least in the context of works produced by students. How does one understand this? One aspect of this quietude is a real reluctance among art students to directly engage with religion as a category of analysis or representation in their work. It is possible to perceive a structural institutional vigilance that keeps check not merely on the content but also modes of representation. The nature of this vigilance is complex: it is not simple repression of the artistic endeavours of students but an incessant panopticon watchfulness that engenders self-discipline on the part of students, reconfiguring their art practice. In another context, talking about art production in 2001, Gulammohammed Sheikh has argued: "When fear is instilled in our lives, we avoid doing some things, or saying some things, of our own accord ...."[11] It is possible that the spectre of the viewing public haunts the FFA such that certain subjects are steered clear of. Nilima Sheikh perspicaciously comments on self-censorship; a constant self-review that renders redundant any scrutiny committee.[12] Nevertheless, Vasudevan Akkitham talks about attempts, both at the Faculty as well as by its alumni, to persist with the broadly left ideological traditions put in place at the FFA.[13]

While the sense of alertness which today marks the FFA has politicized it in a way that it is aware of the ideological field in which it is situated, it has also led to another shift. Wary of the sustained public scrutiny, the FFA has turned inwards, maintaining

only minimally the tenuous but often affectionate relationship it has had with the city. An exclusiveness around the artist and art practice which centres on the Romantic idea of the isolated visionary plays a role here. Other institutional practices which once sought to forge connections with the city have thinned out; the latest announcement regarding the discontinuance of the Fine Arts Fair, long a symbol of the synergy between the Faculty and the city, is an index of this.[14]

The art community that has grown in Baroda had always been Faculty-centred; now with the inward turn these links are somewhat more fragile, says K.P. Reji, FFA alumnus and Baroda-based artist.[15] He also suggests that the intellectual life of the community has become impoverished as a consequence of this inward turn. The general quieting of the FFA can be read in the absence of General Body Meetings of Faculty students, the avoidance of the social, the lack of connection between the FFA and the city, says B.V. Suresh.[16] As Zitzewitz remarks, "... self-consciousness about the secularity of art has become a crucial part of the training of artists and students of art history, alike. Those guards upon expression not only encourage artists to avoid the religious image, but they also put pressure on the art world to become even more exclusive."[17]

Yet, these very guards upon expression do not always preclude the absence of engagement. In fact it is possible that new visual languages can be self-consciously devised that bypass the systematic vigilance of the viewing public.

6a & b
Pamphlets distributed in the run-up to the 2003 Gujarat Assembly elections, using visuals by FFA students. The captions say: (6a) "Increase the size of the state government cabinet, decrease the number of jobs" and (6b) "Listen to our voice: Education, pollution, water, hunger, safety." Photographs: Rashmimala Devi.

Notes

1   For a detailed account of events of May 9, 2007 and after see http://fineartsfacultymsu.blogspot. in (accessed November 2, 2014).

2   Shivaji Panikkar who was Head, Department of Art History and Aesthetics during that period, comments: "Our argument was that art history as a discipline had an inherent potential to grow, take up/address various issues and contemporary questions. We always valued the intrinsic methodologies (formalism to iconology) of Art History as useful along with newer frameworks." Personal communication, December 2014.

3   Karin Zitzewitz, "On Signature and Citizenship: Further Notes on the 'Husain Affair'", in Shivaji K. Panikkar, Parul Dave Mukherji and Deeptha Achar, eds., *Towards A New Art History: Studies in Indian Art*, New Delhi: D.K. Printworld, 2003, pp. 276–87.

4   See *On MF Husain*, New Delhi: SAHMAT, 2011, for a detailed exposition of some of SAHMAT's arguments.

5   For an extended discussion on the "creative nature" of students' protest and its double function, see Akhilesh Arya et al., "Media, City and the 'Fine Artie': Notes on the Student Protest at Faculty of Fine Arts, MS University of Baroda", in Deeptha Achar and Shivaji K. Panikkar, eds., *Articulating Resistance: Art and Activism*, New Delhi: Tulika, 2012, pp. 3–16.

6   Quoted in Raghu Karnad and Shruti Ravindran, "Totem and Taboo", *Outlook India,* May 28, 2007, http://www.outlookindia.com/article/Totem-And-Taboo/234716 (accessed November 1, 2014).

7   Small acts, such as refusal to rent out paying-guest lodgings to Fine Arts students, and refusal to rent out farashkhana shamianas (camping tents or awnings) to the striking students, are a few of the hostile gestures that FFA students had to deal with.

8   Girish Karnad, "This Is No Minor Episode", *Outlook India*, May 15, 2007, http://www. outlookindia.com/article/This-Is-No-Minor-Episode/234646 (accessed November 1, 2014).

9   "VHP Forces MSU to Remove 'Objectionable' Lord Shiva Paintings, Artist Shuts Exhibition", Express News Service, *The Indian Express* (Vadodara), December 29, 2012, p. 3.

10 "Emblem Painting Stirs Row at MSU, Congress Workers Alleged Aseem-Like Work Insults National Symbol", Times News Network, *The Times of India* (Ahmedabad), September 15, 2012, p. 3.

11 "Gulammohammed Sheikh in Conversation with Kavita Singh", in *Gulammohammed Sheikh: Palimpsest*, exhibition catalogue, New Delhi: Vadehra Art Gallery, 2001.

12 Personal interview with Nilima Sheikh, August 2014.

13 Personal interview with Vasudevan Akkitham, August 2014.

14 The VadFest, a four-day extravaganza planned by the Gujarat state government in Baroda during the Republic Day celebrations in January 2015, sees the FFA taking a prominent role in the proceedings. This, however, does not preclude the general quieting of the FFA.

15 Personal interview with K.P. Reji, July 2014.

16 Personal interview with B.V. Suresh, August 2014.

17 Karin Zitzewitz, *The Art of Secularism: The Cultural Politics of Modernist Art in Contemporary India*, Delhi: Oxford University Press, 2014, p. 154.

In Place of a Conclusion: Cosmopolitan and Secular vs Parochial and Communal

Shivaji K. Panikkar

The collection of essays presented here has attempted to throw light upon the historical evolution of Baroda as a unique location from its early becoming of a recognizable provenance within the conditions associated with a princely colonial town. The pre-modern princely state is then propelled into the position of a modern centre of art and craft education, production and viewing; Baroda thus becomes a provenance with the attributes of a distinct sphere of cultural practices. In this evolution, among other things, Baroda is seen here as a location with its own kind of hybrid, assimilative urbanism reflected in its architecture, changing patterns of governance and institutions of culture – of art, craft and architecture – and as a site of networking with the world, and of developing ideas and discourses. All through, as a focal point of its unfolding, there is a sense of the makers acting out their pragmaticism, which makes pre-Independence Baroda a recognizable art-production centre or a provenance reflective of more prominent centres such as Madras, Calcutta or Bombay. Today, as the scholarship on provenance is maturing, perhaps it is time to take up a comparative study of the major and minor colonial centres from the perspective of their formation.

The volume as a whole narrates and interprets the several dynamics of making the provenance of Baroda through the pre-modern, modern and contemporary time-frames. It investigates how the concerns emerging out of the claims of cosmopolitanism become a complex problematic when viewed through the lenses of multiple references, perspectives and methodologies. Further, the essays keep abreast of developments and explore how different understandings and proposals of the site/s can mean either the city of Baroda and/ or its cultural institutions, chiefly Kalabhavan and the Faculty of Fine Arts; and how these sites lend critical or contentious meanings to art practices in varied historical circumstances.

In such a large sweep the volume maps out and brings into view the conduit of development from colonialism through progressive modernism, nationalism and internationalism, leading to the search for a modern indigenous identity. First, Baroda evolves as a significant part of the conception of the integrated nation-state. Here, it is at once a site as well as a case-study to understand the uniqueness of the vernacular, the provincial or even the parochial and communal. In turn, the aspirational values of cosmopolitanism and universalism, worked out through the absorption of the international and the global, become part of the project of evolving from the colonial to the national-modern. However, the fact that one needs to look beyond the nation as a singular, unitary complex is underlined to gesture towards unique provincial locales, which are necessary to the imagination and sustenance of a national culture. Thus, the question of how the art and culture of the locale aspires to align with the larger cosmopolitan world through the national is the concern of most of the narratives herein. Various matrices are taken up for analysis, apart from the very main thematic, i.e. the aspect of cosmopolitanism of the city. A few exceptional matrices are the ones that conceptualize the relationship of locale on one hand with nation, and simultaneously with the macro aspects of the world.

Compared to the earlier singular major attempt[1] to narrate the development of art in the city, this volume expands scholarship on Baroda in a thematically focused manner, through inclusion of developments of the last two decades and shifts in interpretation. The writers effectively inform us of the rooted discourses on ideology, the emergence of politically-edged radical subjectivities and the entry of global impulses of production and distribution, all of which lead to the near disconnect of the artists and their art from the locale of production. These sudden shifts coincide with the rise of majoritarian political sway, which gives the globalizing tendency a peculiar parochial twist. Thus majoritarian forces become responsible for charting a different course for the FFA and artistic practices in Baroda.

Given the specificity of the relationship of the nation with its linguistic territories, the definitional premise of the FFA and the locus of the discourses therein had been a progressive, inclusive and tolerant cosmopolitanism that held forth the universal humanist values of the secular. The systemic impeachments of these very ideals in recent decades are a point of concern in the volume. It is ironical that when this provenance was constructed, the policies of the forward-looking Maharaja Sayajirao III ensured that high-art practitioners, artisans and small industry workers alike flourished. That spirit of inclusion was remarkable through the colonial and nationalist periods. In contrast, in the economically liberalized India of today the dominant political forces choose to silence art practitioners and institutions, making the idea of the original, cosmopolitan and inclusive spirit of the city an irony. A volume like this is welcome as it inaugurates a recognition of the need for deeper interrogations to understand the specific political currents that affect art-making and viewing. One can hope that future researches may be informed by these attempts.

The inevitable question poses itself: how can a locus that enshrines noble national values become a site of variance and of political conflict? Firstly, the *definitional premise* pointed out above should not be understood as a reductionist and oversimplified representation of the site as historically conflict-free. Instead, the history of conflicts and confrontations must engage us as a problematic since these directions are complex and folded over into each other. While keeping in view the instances of oppositionality, dissent and confrontations, FFA as a site and Baroda as a whole still may impress us in a casual glance as an apparently normal, non-conflictual, non-politicized, convivialist habitus where seemingly "pure" or "true" art and culture is taught, learnt, practised and exhibited. This is the facade that is constantly projected as a core value, and promoted by the current administration. How the situation historically played out, and the subtle but decisive shifts in these clusters of thought, need to evolve as full-fledged topics of study, taking forward the initial headway made in this direction by some of the chapters of this book.

1

K.P. Krishnakumar in his Sama studio sculpting model-artist Rekha Rodwittiya, 1986. Photograph: Shivaji Panikkar. Photograph courtesy and copyright: Rekha Rodwittiya.

"New Art History"

To analyse the above premises through art history, we must engage with the discipline's frameworks. Priya Maholay-Jaradi points out: "This volume is conceived against the busy backdrop of a recasting of the discipline of art history, which has been underway in the last two decades in postcolonial nation-states such as India. The discipline earlier enjoyed a predominantly Eurocentric formulation which … promoted dichotomies such as centre-periphery, national-colonial, national-provincial and pure/modern-derivative; in contrast, the current recasting of art history chooses to collapse these dichotomies and present their domains as negotiating and constituting each other."

Explicating the claim of "recasting", I would like to note that art-historical researches on provenance – which included the development of the cultural spheres of specific regions and of the traditional and modern periods – were undertaken at the Department of Art History and Aesthetics, FFA, through 1980–90. This partially resulted from the fact that a majority of students came from other linguistic regions/states, and were likely to return there as artists or teachers in art schools. Some work in that line, at the post-graduate level, was initiated by Ratan Parimoo and continued after his retirement. Sheikh's edited book on the modern art history of Baroda was an innovative example in this direction. However, these art-historical frameworks were largely based on formalism, descriptive studies of iconography, or narrative, iconological and chronology-based surveys of regional developments. Art criticism, being seen as a domain of contemporary art practices, was far removed from art history, though the gap was an artificial one.[2] Given this scenario, the formulation of a "New Art History" in Baroda at the turn of the century focused on developing a framework-oriented approach to replace the object-based approach. The frameworks could be informed by themes such as gender, caste etc. "New" also pointed towards an attempt at *politicization* of the discipline, one that aimed at *intervention* and an *opening out* into historical praxis to become inclusive and discursive.

2
Hoarding for VadFest, Old City, December 2014.

So, the discipline was already being recast keeping in view the shifts in contemporary political assertions. However, Gujarat 2002 was a turning point in the way some of us in the academic world thought about our practice. It was difficult to engage with "pure art history"[3] anymore, in the face of gruesome realities. Considering the elite underpinnings of the discipline in India, it was necessary to make major paradigmatic shifts to allow the discipline to engage with the historical context. The new approach stressed the subjective and ideological position of the researcher. It was an act of resistance that enabled the 2004 conference titled *The Issues of Activism: The Artist and the Historian* in the Department of Art History and Aesthetics, and the publication that followed.[4] Subsequent conferences too maintained a consistency, and art history's role in the training of artists was increasingly revisited. It is necessary to consider why the project of reinventing and politicizing the discipline was discarded as an unfinished project and why the institution was pushed back to its previous disciplinary orientations. The rightwing intervention, in curbing the cosmopolitan and the secular has indeed diminished the possibility of art history in India keeping abreast with international trends. The role of the university administration, the vernacular press and the majoritarian state power is crucial to an understanding of this failure of the institution.[5] Since then, the FFA has introduced self-financed graduate and post-graduate programmes in Design[6] and has participated in the first ever VadFest 2015.[7]

Events such as the above may be interpreted as corrective means to restore lost reputation by the Faculty administration. All the same, the institution negotiates (with the dominant political will that celebrates global capital) and tries to survive in the changing circumstances. A bit of retrospection reveals how much Baroda has been changed by the events starting on May 9, 2007, and it is perhaps time to reflect on the events from a historical perspective. It would be useful to understand the idea of the "political" in relation to "art practice" as far as the Baroda scene is concerned. Further, we may ask how a shift from secular to communal creates new conditions that impinge on art-making and art language in the city.

3
VHP mob at the FFA gates, May 14, 2007.
Photograph: Atreyee Gupta.

Shifting Languages: The Political and the Subjective

Karin Zitzewitz notes, "Sheikh's painting helped me to realize that while my initial impression of the city's cosmopolitanism was not false, it must coexist with the ethics and politics that produce communal violence."[8] She elaborates on the deep impact of the 1969 communal violence in Gujarat and the way it politicized Gulammohammed Sheikh's paintings through autobiographic reflection via the city.[9]

The above is a distinct development, considering that from the early Bengal School/Revivalist phase of the 1890s, through Santiniketan and the period of mid-20th-century internationalism, to the decade of the 1970s, art in India was for the most part defined *away* from the political,[10] and premised on cultural-nationalism, in tandem with the liberational political fervour of the new nation-state. Expectedly, the artistic choice and spirit of the newly formed art school of Baroda was for a formalist-international-modernism[11] that tangentially based itself on the Nehruvian vision of progress and an acceptance of the best of the world. "Progressive" meant moving ahead of the *traditionalisms*, the *colonial* and the *status-quo/canonical* nature of existing cultural practices. Artists of Baroda travelled widely, experiencing modern and contemporary art around the world.[12]

Simultaneously, the same generation was critiqued for *derivative* art practices, which led to the search for a certain *authenticity* based on national/regional identity. Thus, the initial impetus of international modernism gave way to a quest for a rootedness in the indigenous culture/s in the 1960s–70s. As a result, within an engagement with locale, a position that moved against universalist abstraction was seen, especially in the works of Gulammohammed Sheikh and Bhupen Khakhar.[13] While sources from living folk traditions were explored, simultaneously Sheikh's pedagogical initiative privileged narration and figuration over abstraction.[14] This was a crucial step which endured through the 1970s–80s, until Sheikh's voluntary retirement from the FFA in the early 1990s. Just as this engagement with "living traditions" prolonged engagement with location-specific figuration and narration, and art-making and teaching practices were ongoing at FFA, Baroda marked swift shifts in the 1980s.[15]

The laidback '70s became the polemical '80s. Baroda's intellectual climate enabled constant dialogues between artists and art critics/historians, and often students. These two decades were crucial for the FFA, as several Baroda artists began expressing themselves through an art based on their ideologically bound, radical subjectivities. A changed understanding of the *political* developed from the mid-'80s. While art in the previous decades had been more formal and impersonal, now artists' subjectivities were seen developing under various rubrics: feminist (Nilima Sheikh, Rekha Rodwittiya, Pushpamala N.), gay (Khakhar), communitarian (Gulam Sheikh, Jyoti Bhatt), class- and caste-based (K.P. Krishnakumar, K. Prabhakaran, N.N. Rimzon), and in other directions chosen by members of the Indian Radical Painters & Sculptors Association (IRP&SA). As the very notion of the political was redefined, the art world also displayed major shift-overs.[16]

During the second half of the 1980s through the early '90s to the present, some of the newly recruited painter-teachers at FFA, i.e. Vasudevan Akkitham, B.V. Suresh, Rekha Rodwittiya, Indrapramit Roy and Sashidharan, who were initially trained in the narrative idiom, undid much of their Baroda schooling and acquired a more open-ended pictorial vocabulary.[17] Since the mid-1980s, the collage-palimpsest mode of breaking narrative continuities and exploration of various pictorial sensibilities, along with the unprecedented

4
Wet Field, by Vasudevan Akkitham, 1990.
Oil on canvas, 173 x 173 cm. Courtesy of
Osian's Archive & Library Collection.

5
Painted Bird 2, by B.V. Suresh, 1990. Soft
pastels on cartridge paper, 53.3 x 73.6 cm.
Photograph: B.V. Suresh.

experimentations in spatial forms and mediums, have been crucial to art practice in Baroda.
This can be seen as the breakaway point that relates to contemporary developments in an
art language that pays less attention to Baroda-based events – what Santhosh Sadanand
points out as artists' near disconnect from their locale.

This is in contrast to the ideological orientation that informed art events enabled by
Sheikh in the later part of the '70s and early '80s with FFA as a centre; *Place for People*
(1981) was one such prime event.[18] FFA alumnus Vivan Sundaram who developed a
self-proclaimed leftist ideology and iconography in the mid-1960s was one major artist
who was political and painted in response to the Emergency.[19] Sundaram's collaboration
with Bombay-based artists Sudhir Patwardhan and Nalini Malani, and the art critic Geeta
Kapur, shared the avant-garde intention, and FFA's numerous activities promoted ideas of
a politically rooted, relevant figuration and development of historical narratives.[20]

Place for People was a culmination of such politicizing trends using narrativity, social
iconography and historical reflexivity. Several other shifts also emerged simultaneously –
one such was the mobilizing of the "personal" that could be read across the contemporary
gay and feminist social and political movements. With this Khakhar's art moved quickly
to the release of the unspoken, assuming a bizarre realism so far unfamiliar to the art
world. Feminist ideology similarly enabled subjectivity in Rekha Rodwittiya's development
of iconography which dealt with a violent and expressionist thematic. Pushpamala N.'s
autobiographically-centred terracotta sculptures articulated the inner-recesses of the girl-
child in an odd, amusing and celebrative mode. Senior artists like Nilima Sheikh too
narrativized their personal concerns about social issues such as bride burning.

Cumulatively, the above exhibits and the inaugural show of the IRP&SA, *Questions &
Dialogues* (March 1987), made the art scene at FFA highly polemical. Artistic disagreements,

particularly with the immediately older generation, and greater interaction within the younger generation, led to significant exhibits and arguments at *Questions & Dialogues*.[21] Globalization was becoming a reality, and this was the time the art market and art galleries were finding their foothold in metropolises like Bombay and Delhi. The first ever-global art auction in the country was held in Bombay, and it is significant that the IRP&SA staged a protest against this.[22]

So far art discourses were contained within the art fraternity. The rise of majoritarian politics and its violent modes of intervention in the second half of the 1980s, leading up to the current scenario through the events of May 2007, is where the very premise of the cosmopolitanism of FFA and of Baroda begins to be questionable. The earliest instances of such intervention were experienced in the late 1980s through early 1990s. Under Sheikh's initiative, FFA students were involved in producing lithographic prints of anti-communal posters which were pasted in the Old City. Following this, the Vadodara Shanti Abhiyan (Baroda Peace Campaign) was formed by concerned citizens from various walks of life, including faculty members of different departments of the M.S. University, artists and activists such as Sheikh and Khakhar.[23] The artistic provenance that belonged to a negligible number of the art fraternity suddenly seemed to call the attention of the larger public. The events that led to the voluntary retirement of Sheikh[24] had a national-level ramification in the M.F. Husain affair. These were surely lessons being taught and learnt by the artist community, while Baroda's public began to affiliate with majoritarian rightwing politics. There are certain meanings that could be read across these developments: the tightening grip of majoritarian politics over the FFA; a shift in artists' language to a more generic, non-committal choice of themes; their disengagement with the locale and consequently greater alignment with a metropolitan/global art market.

There could be two major fallouts of the rise of majoritarian politics and its interventions in the cultural field. First, fear is instilled in artists' minds, so that contentious issues,

6
Famous Mrs G, by Vivan Sundaram, 1974. Oil on canvas, 175.8 x 155.2 cm. Courtesy of Osian's Archive & Library Collection.

7
How Naked Shall I Stand For You, by Rekha Rodwittiya, 1985. Watercolour, gouache and graphite pencil on paper, 183 x 91.5 cm. Collection: Chester and Davida Herwitz, Peabody Essex Museum, Salem, Massachusetts. Photograph: Jyoti Bhatt.

8
Girl with Shell, by Pushpamala N., 1985. Terracotta with engobe painting, approximate height 91.5 cm. Collection: Jal Aria, Mumbai. Photograph: Ashish Rajadhyaksha.

religious images or obvious sexual displays are totally avoided. And if attempted at all, such themes become clothed in metaphoric or allegoric language, or are hidden within other less contentious subjects. Or the artist may simply resort to the purely experiential aesthetic of violence so that the work is not read as questioning the majoritarian position. The second, and more consequential outcome of the communalized situation is when a section of the art community begins to wage a proxy war against the now infamous "pseudo-secularists" – the facelessness and non-self-identification of such rightwing players making the institutional space of art apparently conflict-free. However such polarization has existed since 1989–91; it is obvious that some students and members of the faculty at FFA have partisanship with rightwing politics, a fact more in evidence after the May 2007 events.

When Art Finally Meets the Public: Questions and No Dialogues

Kwame Anthony Appiah suggests the possibility of a cosmopolitan community in which individuals from varying locations (physical, economic etc.) enter relationships of mutual respect despite their differing beliefs (religious, political etc.).[25] As the publication *Articulating Resistance: Art and Activism* was taking shape there was a growing disbelief in the possibility that art could unify the world as a cosmopolitan community. Questions were raised, such as what art or artists can do to change the course of political events, what the responsibilities of the art community are, and whether it is capable of doing anything substantial in the face of communal violence or physical attacks on artists. I would like to argue at the end of this essay, which is by way of a conclusion to the volume, that it is precisely the intolerance emerging from majoritarian politics that negates the cosmopolitan proposition. The modern art world surely belongs to the enlightened urban context, but indeed there exists a wide gap between the world of fine art and the public in general, there is virtually no sociality between these realms; this is true for Baroda as well as other Indian urban centres. But for exceptional individuals and some among the wealthy and distinguished, very few people (even among the university community) take any active interest in "fine arts". As a result there has been very little of what may be seen as "commonly shared values" between the world of art and of the public. On the one hand, the diverse multicultural FFA was surely participatory, and it represented the multiplicity of the Indian nation-state; but again, the disconnect of the art world with its locale is a reality.

The questioning extends itself to the presumption of an undivided art community. As we reconcile with artists divided along political lines, what has changed is significant – say in post-2007 Baroda or after the M.F. Husain incident. As the post-2007 students' strikes were brought to closure and the situation at the FFA was being "normalized" it was difficult to reconcile oneself with the fact that there wasn't a unified art community that could stand together with a minimum agenda in resisting the rightwing's control of the overall functioning of the institution. Resistance movements have hardly been able to achieve anything substantial. Slowly but steadily the institution is taken over,

9
When Champa Grew Up (a series of 12 paintings), by Nilima Sheikh, 1984. Gum tempera on vasli paper, 30.5 x 40.5 cm each. Collection: New Walk Museum and Art Gallery, Leicester, UK.

10a & b
Artists against Communalism posters made by FFA students with Gulammohammed Sheikh, 1990–91. Translation: (left) Communal Harmony Day / January 30, 1991 / Near Gandhi Nagar Gruh / Prayer, Paintings, Street Play / Evening 5 to 7. / Dhrupad Music / Ustad Fariduddin Khan Dagar / Home Science Auditorium / Evening 7.30; (right) *Himsa band karo* (Stop the violence). Lithographic prints. Collection: Gulammohammed Sheikh.

11
Striking students with banners, posters and placards, FFA, May 14, 2007. Photograph: Chandramohan.

12
Artists against Communalism with SAHMAT at Mahatma Gandhi Nagar Gruh, 1991. In the front row facing the camera: second from right, Rajkumar Hans; fourth from right, Professor Chandrashekhar; fifth from right, Gulammohammed Sheikh; in the second row first from right (mauve sari) Gita Bajpai. Photograph courtesy Gulammohammed Sheikh.

13
Banner of Artists against Communalism with SAHMAT and Vadodara Shanti Abhiyan (Baroda Peace Campaign), at Mahatma Gandhi Nagar Gruh, 1991. Painted at Bhupen Khakhar's residence, the banner carries a verse by the saint-poet of medieval India, Kabir: *Aisi bani boliye, manka aapa khoy; auronko sheetal karein, aap bhi sheetal hoy* (Speak such words, sans ego and anger, that the self and the listener experience calm). Photograph courtesy Gulammohammed Sheikh.

and virtually all aspects of artists' work – from the practice of nude study to what can be exhibited – are controlled; and in the place of freedom of expression and autonomy what exists is fear, so that most choices of self-expression are made redundant.

Notes
1   Gulammohammed Sheikh, ed., *Contemporary Art in Baroda*, New Delhi: Tulika, 1997.
2   Editors' "Introduction", in Shivaji K. Panikkar, Parul Dave Mukherji and Deeptha Achar, eds., *Towards A New Art History: Studies in Indian Art*, New Delhi: D.K. Printworld, 2003, pp. 50–56.
3   Conventional art history that undertakes formalism as its primary tool; this is a descriptive and object-based approach, totally devoid of any ideological/subjective orientation, and in terms of methodology claims scientific objectivity.
4   Deeptha Achar and Shivaji K. Panikkar, eds., *Articulating Resistance: Art and Activism*, New Delhi: Tulika, 2012.
5   As such, the physical appearance of FFA has been changing drastically since the events of May 2007. In my recent visit to FFA it struck me that the campus was being given a makeover to assume an all-new corporate look, with very neatly defined pathways and new lawns urgently being laid-out. While the spaces are given this thoroughly new facade, the students and faculty informed me of a lowering in the quality of education since the rightwing entry, and the "normalizing" thereafter.
6   These are integrated courses with inputs of crafts and design, ceramics and glass, moving images, communication design and accessory design.
7   VadFest 2015 is a festival with 50 events, across 15 venues; its website (http://vadfest.com/) pitches it as one of India's biggest multi-arts, multi-venue culture festivals; an experience that will stay with one forever. "VadFest 2015 is an international art and culture festival spread across the

four-day Republic Day weekend – from January 23rd to 26th. Legends from across India and around the world will grace the cityscape for a fabulous four-day celebration of art, music, dance, drama, culture, food and a special kids' theater fest."

8 Karin Zitzewitz, *The Art of Secularism: The Cultural Politics of Modernist Art in Contemporary India,* Delhi: Oxford University Press, 2014, p. 102.

9 It can be seen that autobiographical referentiality was one of the methods adopted by Bhupen Khakhar and Gulam Sheikh, along with the method of metaphoric and allegoric encodings, which demanded a reading of the painting literarily/textually.

10 An exceptional instance of political art in the country was the art produced under the Communist Party, particularly in the context of the Bengal Famine of 1942–43 and thereafter.

11 Since its inception FFA's art pedagogy was based on international modern ideas, and this was liberating as it departed from two established credos: first, the narrow parochial/national/revivalist option and second, the academic/colonial. The idea of internationalism in art language perhaps gives an impression of the liberal, cosmopolitan values at the FFA. The art world in general had always been liberal, secular, international, creative, sympathetic and yet largely non-political. Primarily this internationalism was about modernist formalism or about simplifying or abstracting images in their representation, and meant cultivation of skills and methods for modernist form-making such as in the case of Sankho Chaudhuri, N.S. Bendre and others.

12 It is necessary to keep in view that many artist-teachers like K.G. Subramanyan, G.M. Sheikh, Ratan Parimoo, Jyoti Bhatt and Raghav Kaneria, among others, travelled to Europe and America during the 1950s–80s; these travels had tremendous impact on their worldview and ideology as well as their art practice and pedagogy. The artist-teacher Nasreen Mohamedi was trained abroad; the travels and study of artists and art critics outside the FFA, such as Bhupen Khakhar, Vivan Sundaram and Geeta Kapur, and their association with the Faculty definitely influenced and shaped art thinking at the institution.

13 Between 1969 and 1973 the "little art journal" *Vrishchik* was published from Baroda, edited by Sheikh and Khakhar. In the early '70s Geeta Kapur's seminal essay "In Quest of Identity" was published in it.

14 The 1960s–70s, through pioneers like K.G. Subramanyan (and J. Swaminathan through Group 1890) had effectively brought about a critique of Western influences; all the same, questions of national identity in art languages began to be resolved through historically and contemporaneously available indigenous sources or "living traditions".

15 There was a rooted cosmopolitanism that developed in the works of senior artists like Khakhar and Sheikh. Khakhar's thematic of gay disclosure was inspired by the international gay liberation movement and its reflection in art and life abroad.

16 I am referring to the shifts from an abstraction-based art-making, particularly such as the sculptures of Nagji Patel, to a range of figuration based on pop-realism as in the works of Ravindra Reddy, Dhruv Mistry and Prithipal Singh Ladi in the late 1970s, and major shift-overs through the '80s with the works of Pushpamala N., N.N. Rimzon and Alex Mathew, among others.

17 The breakaway was marked by dispensing with the credos of abstraction and figuration and this was, perhaps, largely a result of their study/stay/travel in Europe through the late '80s and early '90s. Earliest from the younger generation to receive the Inlaks scholarship and study at the Royal College of Art, London, was Dhruv Mistry (1981–83), followed by Rekha Rodwittiya (1982–84), B.V. Suresh (1985–87), Vasudevan Akkitham (1986–88) and Indrapramit Roy (1989–91).

18 *Place for People*, Jehangir Art Gallery, Bombay, November 9–15, 1981, and Rabindra Bhavan,

New Delhi, November 21–December 3, 1981. The exhibition included artists Jogen Chowdhury, Bhupen Khakhar, Nalini Malani, Sudhir Patwardhan, Gulammohammed Sheikh and Vivan Sundaram. Geeta Kapur wrote the catalogue essay.

19 Sheikh's painting too reflected the crisis, so also the work of artist Jyoti Bhatt.

20 The participation of art historian Timothy Hyman and filmmakers like Kumar Shahani, the seminars and art workshops at Kasauli Art Centre and publication of the *Journal of Arts and Ideas* are related to such a formation and alignment.

21 Artists visited each other's studios regularly. Artists like K.P. Krishnakumar and Rodwittiya articulated their radical views; the short teaching assignment of the dynamic, aggressive and assertive Rodwittiya was discontinued by the authorities. The manifesto of the group, largely articulated by Anita Dube, yearned for a praxis based on liberation from the existing elite art production and viewing system; it presented a critique of postmodernist art production and its avoidance of any serious examination of the politics of visual culture and content; it took a critical stand in conjunction with its nascent desire and search for alternative practices through art.

The exhibition and the accompanying manifesto, written by Dube, and the posters that were put up in the campus, gave rise to unease and debate at the open discussion during the show. The aggressive self-conscious radical polemic of the group that came through in the booklet *Questions & Dialogues* questioned the insincere social commitment of the narrative-figurative artists, reactionary revivalist ideology and in general everything about mainstream art and politics in contemporary Indian art.

22 The group put up a demonstration against the *Timeless Art* exhibition and auction by Sotheby's at Bombay's Victoria Terminus station and printed a pamphlet that scathingly criticized the commercialization of art and artists: "The *Times of India*'s sudden interest in Indian Art and Culture now shows that the Imperialists want to completely poison the people's mind and life through antihuman projects for artists. These are antihuman because with big money they can buy artists and art critics and make them their slaves. The thirty-five artists who are not afraid to sell themselves to the agents of Imperialism don't know that art is not the private property of the mind but the spirit of the whole country." Further, the pamphlet pointed out that it had been the "Colonialist strategy to see everything as 'timeless', and now the Indian ruling classes see their country with the same eyes." *Against Imperialist Exploitation of Art*, IRP&SA, March 10, 1989.

23 SAHMAT gave the name to this anti-communal front.

24 In 1989, following the University Grants Commission (UGC) circular, Sheikh began assigning students to make anti-communalization posters. A few volunteers visited schools to inform children against communalism, and organized meetings. With the intervention of the Vishwa Hindu Parishad, this was deliberately misrepresented in the Gujarati press as communal activity, and Sheikh was accused of initiating it. The bosses of the M.S. University Students Union publicly called for Sheikh to be expelled from the University and a series of related events followed at FFA. Sheikh was finally granted voluntary retirement in 1991.

25 Kwame Anthony Appiah, "Cosmopolitan Patriots", *Critical Inquiry*, Vol. 23, No. 3, Spring 1997, pp. 617–39.

Index

Contributors

Gulammohammed Sheikh is an artist and writer based in Vadodara. He taught History of Art and Painting for nearly three decades at the Faculty of Fine Arts, M.S. University, Baroda. Among his many exhibitions in India and overseas was a significant solo show at Centre Georges Pompidou, Paris, 1985. He has contributed essays to *Marg* and the *Journal of Arts and Ideas*, and edited *Contemporary Art in Baroda* (1997).

Priya Maholay-Jaradi, former Curator at the Asian Civilisations Museum, Singapore, is an independent art historian. She has an MA in art history from SOAS, London and a PhD from the National University of Singapore. She has initiated a post-doctoral project, *Asian Collection Studies* at the IIAS, Leiden (2013). She is the author of *Portrait of a Community: Paintings and Photographs of the Parsees* (2002), *Parsi Portraits from the Studio of Raja Ravi Varma* (2011) and a forthcoming book on Baroda's modernity and nationalism.

Ajay Sinha teaches courses on Asian Art, and Indian Photography and Film at Mount Holyoke College, South Hadley, Massachusetts. He has an MA in art history from M.S. University, Baroda, and a PhD from the University of Pennsylvania, Philadelphia. He has published articles on India's ancient religious architecture and modern and contemporary art, authored *Imagining Architects: Creativity in Indian Temple Architecture* (2000) and co-edited *Bollyworld: Popular Indian Cinema through a Transnational Lens* (2005).

Christopher W. London specializes in the history of Indian architecture during the 19th and 20th centuries. He has a DPhil in Modern History from Oriel College, Oxford University. He has edited two Marg volumes, *Architecture in Victorian and Edwardian India* (1994) and *The Arts of Kutch* (2000), and contributed to three others – *Bombay to Mumbai* (1997), *Lucknow: Then and Now* (2003) and *Banaras: The City Revealed* (2005). His book *Bombay Gothic* (2002) is now in a second edition (2012).

Ratan Parimoo has a PhD from M.S. University, Baroda, where he also taught for 34 years, serving as Head of the Department of Art History and Aesthetics (1966–91) and as Dean of the Faculty of Fine Arts (1975–81). Among his numerous publications are *Paintings of the Three Tagores* (1973), republished in an expanded version as *Art of Three Tagores: From Revival to Modernity* (2010), and *Historical Development of Contemporary Indian Art* (2009). Since 2007 he has been the Director of the L.D. Museum and N.C. Mehta Art Gallery, Ahmedabad.

Karin Zitzewitz teaches Art History and Visual Culture at Michigan State University, Ann Arbor. She has a PhD in anthropology from Columbia University, New York. She is the author of *The Perfect Frame: Presenting Modern Indian Art: Stories and Photographs from the Kekoo Gandhy Collection* (2003) and *The Art of Secularism: The Cultural Politics of Modernist Art in Contemporary India* (2014).

Chithra K.S. is a museologist based in Bangalore, with a PhD from M.S. University, Baroda. She is currently working with Tasveer Foundation, Bangalore. She has been involved in curatorial and research projects with Jackfruit Research and Designs (2006–09) and the Asia Art Archive (2011–14). She received the Victoria and Albert Museum UK Visiting Fellowship (2013).

Rashmimala Devi is a practising artist based in Baroda with MFA degrees in Painting and Art Criticism from M.S. University, Baroda. She has exhibited extensively, including at the *Kochi-Muziris Biennale Collateral Group Show*, 2013, and has been involved in mural projects such as the prestigious *Conjuring Lands* for the Mumbai International Airport as well as children's book illustration.

Sabih Ahmed completed the interdisciplinary MA programme at the School of Arts and Aesthetics, Jawaharlal Nehru University, New Delhi, in 2009. He is a Senior Researcher at Asia Art Archive. Based in New Delhi, he has overseen numerous research initiatives that include digitization projects such as The Baroda Archives and the digitized personal archive of Geeta Kapur and Vivan Sundaram. He has also spearheaded with his colleagues in the Archive an ongoing Bibliography project that charts the history of art-writing in 13 Indian languages.

Santhosh S. is Assistant Professor at the School of Culture and Creative Expressions, Ambedkar University, Delhi. His area of work is in the field of critical historiography of Indian art-historical studies, institutional formations and cultural practices in relation to minoritarian politics, on which he has published several essays. He was previously Visiting Faculty at the School of Arts and Aesthetics, Jawaharlal Nehru University, New Delhi.

Chaitanya Sambrani is an art historian and curator with degrees in Art Criticism (MA) from M.S. University, Baroda, and Art History and Curatorship (PhD) from Australian National University, Canberra. He is currently Senior Lecturer in the Centre for Art History and Art Theory at the ANU School of Art. He has curated and authored *Edge of Desire: Recent Art in India* (2005) among several other projects.

Deeptha Achar teaches at the Department of English, M.S. University, Baroda. She has a PhD from the Central Institute of English and Foreign Languages, Hyderabad. She has co-edited, among others, *Towards a New Art History: Studies in Indian Art* (2003), *Discourse, Democracy and Difference* (2010) and *Articulating Resistance: Art and Activism* (2012). Her research interests include childhood studies, visual culture and the history of education in India.

Shivaji K. Panikkar is currently Professor at the School of Culture and Creative Expressions, Ambedkar University, Delhi. With MA and PhD degrees in art history from M.S. University, Baroda, and having taught for over 30 years, he was Head of the Department of Art History and Aesthetics at the University from 2000 to 2007. A prolific writer, he also edited *Twentieth Century Indian Sculpture: The Last Two Decades* (Marg, 2000) and *Towards a New Art History: Studies in Indian Art* (2003).